Seven Metaphors on Management

"The management concepts embodied in the Seven Metaphors provide a practical framework for developing the requisite cultural sensitivities and cross-cultural managerial skills critical for success in the dynamic business environment in the Arab world."

Dr Ray R Irani,
Chairman and Chief Executive Officer,
Occidental Petroleum Corporation

"Muna's metaphors delightfully cover the vital topics for management anywhere. Set as they are in the Arabian Gulf, they offer a unique and powerful insight into the challenges of management in that most critical part of the world."

Susan Vinnicombe,
Professor of Organizational Behaviour and Diversity Management,
Cranfield School of Management, Cranfield University, England

"Dr. Muna has written a most enlightening and thought-provoking book that relates to both business and personal life. He has excelled in his portrayal of the Seven Metaphors by enriching them with his multicultural experience and empirical research. This book provides a fresh insight on human development."

Ted D Abdo,
A founder of Meirc Training & Consulting

"This is a concise and fascinating book covering seven highly practical and visual managerial tools. Seven Metaphors on Management should be required reading for all Arab, expatriate, and multinational managers working with or for Arab organizations."

Faisal M Al Suwaidi,
Vice Chairman and Managing Director,
Qatar Liquefied Gas Company, Qatar

T0270880

Seven Metaphors on Management

Dedicated to the role models in my life so far

My father, Abdallah Muna
My first manager, Lloyd Wickstrom
My mentor, Simon Siksek

Seven Metaphors on Management

Tools for Managers in the Arab World

Farid A Muna

Routledge
Taylor & Francis Group

LONDON AND NEW YORK

First published 2003 by Gower Publishing

Reissued 2018 by Routledge
2 Park Square, Milton Park, Abingdon, Oxon, OX14 4RN
711 Third Avenue, New York, NY 10017

Routledge is an imprint of the Taylor & Francis Group, an informa business

A Library of Congress record exists under LC control number: 2002045238

Typeset in Goudy by LaserScript Ltd, Mitcham, Surrey

ISBN 13: 978-1-138-72617-8 (hbk)
ISBN 13: 978-1-138-72614-7 (pbk)
ISBN 13: 978-1-315-19154-6 (ebk)

Contents

List of figures and tables   ix

Acknowledgements   xi

On metaphors   xiii

Introduction   xv

1 The candle: Ingredients for managerial success   1

2 The iceberg: Competencies and human resources
   management   23

3 The tripod: On motivation and job performance   43

4 The transit lounge: Managing a multicultural staff   59

5 The mosaic: Management in the Arabian Gulf
   countries   75

6 The helicopter: Creative problem solving and decision
    making   101

7 The bridge: Strategic thinking and retirement planning   127

Appendix   157

References   173

Index   177

Figures and tables

Figures

1.1	Ingredients and competencies for managerial success	3
1.2	Upbringing and development	16
3.1	Motivating managers	48
4.1	The onion image of culture	63
4.2	Culture as a normal distribution	65
5.1	Managers and their various environments	78
5.2	Responses for the decision-making styles (2002 study)	87
5.3	Comparison of the *most effective* decision-making styles (1989 and 2002)	88
5.4	Comparison of the *prefer to work under* decision-making styles (1989 and 2002)	89
5.5	Comparison of the *own manager's* decision-making styles (1980, 1989 and 2002)	90
6.1	The deviation diagram	117
6.2	Fishbone diagram for the case of Nader	118

6.3   The Pareto 80–20 chart for the case of Nader   120
6.4   The How-How? diagram for the case of Nader   121
7.1   Four phases to building the strategy bridge   131
7.2   The five phases of retirement   146
7.3   Age and happiness   149
7.4   Core values and age   153
7.5   A balanced scorecard for retirement   155

Tables

4.1a Expatriates as perceived by Gulf managers, *most
       admired* characteristics   70
4.1b Expatriates as perceived by Gulf managers, *most
       disliked* characteristics   70
5.1   Gulf Cooperation Council population and workforce   81

Acknowledgements

This book is the product of extensive field research; years of interaction with academicians, business leaders and managers; and the "business school of life", as Charles Handy likes to call it. Therefore, I am deeply indebted to all the people who participated in our research; to those managers who attended our courses and seminars; and to all others who knowingly or unknowingly influenced and shaped my way of thinking on business and life. They are too many to mention by name, but they will know whom I mean when they read this book.

I was fortunate to be working with creative and experienced colleagues at Meirc Training & Consulting. I learned a lot from them over the years. I am grateful for those who gave their time and comments during the writing of this book. In particular, thanks to my colleagues Ted Abdo, Ramsey Hakim, and Ziad Zennie for their valuable feedback on the manuscript. In this respect, I am also grateful to my daughter, Nadia Muna, for her useful comments and suggestions on each chapter.

Thanks to Guy Loft of Gower Publishing whose up-front honesty, commitment and professional work turned a manuscript into a book.

I reserve my deepest gratitude and love to the four ladies in my life: my wife Doris, and our three daughters Rima, Nadia and Zeina. They shared the trials and tribulations of my business career that required a lot of travel away from home; they endured (but often enjoyed) the seven different countries in three continents we lived in because of my work. I am now looking forward to spending more quality time with them: I only wish I had done more of it earlier in life.

Farid A Muna
Dana Point, California
November 2002

On metaphors

Metaphor: (met-a-for), a figure of speech in which a word or phrase denoting one kind of object or idea is used in place of another to suggest a likeness or analogy between them.

Time, space and causality are only metaphors of knowledge, with which we explain things to ourselves.

(Friedrich Nietzsche)

Metaphors are much more tenacious than facts.

(Paul Deman)

You don't see something until you have the right metaphor to let you perceive it.

(Thomas S Kuhn)

Introduction

I keep six honest serving-men
(They taught me all I knew);
Their names were What and Why and When
And How and Where and Who.

(Rudyard Kipling)

This book is about seven metaphors that continue to serve me well in my life and business career. I have shared them with business leaders, managers attending our seminars, friends and colleagues, and with my family. Each metaphor is covered in a separate chapter. Let me describe briefly how I came across these metaphors, and what each stands for.

The first metaphor, the *Candle*, was my father's legacy. He used the metaphor of a well-made candle that sheds light to illuminate our journey through life. Unknown to him, he was describing almost exactly what our research discovered many years later about the ingredients for managerial success. The research discovered ten ingredients for success; the first five are described in Chapter 1, and the next five in Chapter 2. The implications of the research findings for child development and for recruitment are also examined. Incidentally, I have always felt that these five ingredients are not necessarily restricted to success in management, but are pertinent to life in general.

The second metaphor, the *Iceberg*, is used by several human resources professionals to describe the competencies one needs to produce outstanding performance in a given area of responsibility. Competencies are a combination of skills, knowledge and attitudes, with skills being the tip of the iceberg. Attitudes, the crucial part of the iceberg, are acquired mostly during childhood and adolescence. Although knowledge and skills are acquired throughout life, the employer plays a major role in that process. Since the next five ingredients for success are also, more or less, initiated and controlled by the employer, their relationship to competencies is covered in this chapter. The application of the competency approach to various human resources functions is also discussed.

The *Tripod* metaphor is one that we, at Meirc Training & Consulting, utilize to examine the often misused and misunderstood concept of motivation. By putting motivation in its larger context of work performance, we are able to appreciate the impact that each of the three legs of the tripod has on motivation, namely, the immediate manager, the corporate culture, and the external environment. The critical role of self-motivation in work performance is vividly highlighted.

The fourth metaphor, the *Transit Lounge*, was inspired by one of the many descriptions of life in the Arabian Gulf Cooperation Council countries[1] where the majority of the population or workforce are expatriates. People from many parts of the world come to the Gulf countries to live and work; some stay long periods, but the majority go back to their countries of origin after only a few years. As we observe the "transit lounge" mindsets in most organizations in the Gulf, it becomes clear that working with and managing people who work for local or multinational companies requires a number of special multicultural skills.

The *Mosaic*, the fifth metaphor, was originally coined by the anthropologist Carleton Coon when he described the Middle East. Communities in the Arab countries are akin to a colorful mosaic made up of overlapping groups and various cultures. Managers and employees at the workplace feel the wider environmental pressures and problems. In this chapter, we take a close look at the recent trends in managerial styles over the past two decades, only to discover that there is a slow drift towards a more democratic style of management. Having been an expatriate myself, I have included a small section entitled "On being an expatriate in the Gulf".

My favorite metaphor is the *Helicopter*. A large international company made the term helicopter view popular when they discovered that their most successful executives possessed this competency. Once again, in life as in business, taking the helicopter view vastly improves one's ability to face crises or solve problems. Although best taught during childhood and early adolescence, the helicopter view is one of the competencies that, once learned, can serve managers well throughout their careers. In addition, this chapter introduces various creative problem-solving and decision-making methods. A hypothetical case study is offered to demonstrate the complete process of problem solving and decision making.

The final chapter covers the seventh metaphor, the *Bridge*. My colleague, Dr. Ramsey Hakim, and I found it to be an excellent management tool when used in strategic thinking and planning. It certainly served us well when facilitating strategy workshops for Arab and international organizations. It describes, systematically and visually, the journey towards the future and across the bridge – starting with the vision statement and ending with a balanced scorecard. The bridge can also be used effectively for retirement planning; a hypothetical retirement case illustrates the planning process.

Although each of the seven chapters is a stand-alone reading, some chapters are closely related; for example, The Candle and The Iceberg cover Meirc's research on the ten ingredients for managerial success. The Transit Lounge and The Mosaic discuss the skills of working with and managing expatriates and Gulf Arabs.

This book is based partly on research studies carried out over a period of two decades. I published the first study in 1980, in a book entitled *The Arab Executive*. Meirc Training & Consulting, carried out the second study, *The Making of Gulf Managers*, in 1989. The present book represents the 2002 update of the main portions of the earlier studies. Therefore, topics such as decision-making styles, environmental pressures and problems, perception of expatriates, and the ten ingredients for managerial success have been revisited and significant trends identified.

This book is also based on my professional and personal experiences in both the West and the Arab world, particularly in the Gulf countries. These experiences relate to my roles as a management consultant and trainer, a practicing manager, and a father. Thus, I have used personal as well as business anecdotes and examples to illustrate some of the points. Finally, the latest international management research and writings were woven into the various chapters where appropriate.

Some readers may wonder why I chose *seven* metaphors. What is so magical about the number seven? Well, back in 1956 psychologist George A. Miller wrote an interesting article entitled "The Magical Number Seven, Plus or Minus Two: Some Limits on Our Capacity for Processing Information". Miller suggested that the number seven reflects our cognitive makeup; he concluded that seven is about the number of categories of information that we can comfortably retain in our immediate memory. He said, "The span of absolute judgment and the span of immediate memory impose severe limitations on the amount of information that we are able to receive, process, and remember." Miller provided the examples of the Seven Wonders of the World, seven days of the week, the seven primary colors, the seven notes of the musical scale, and the seven seas. He concludes, "Perhaps there is something deep and profound behind all these sevens, something just calling out for us to discover it."

Maybe this phenomenon provided me with an excuse for choosing only seven metaphors in order to leave room for future reflections!

Like Kipling's honest serving-men, I hope that these metaphors will teach us a few new, and some old, things; about bringing up children; managing human resources; understanding motivation; managing cultural differences; problem solving and decision making; and thinking and planning strategically. One or two of the metaphors will be particularly helpful to Gulf managers and expatriates who are working in the Arabian Gulf countries.

Note

1 The Arabian Gulf Cooperation Council countries are Bahrain, Kuwait, Oman, Qatar, Saudi Arabia, and the United Arab Emirates.

Chapter One

The candle

Ingredients for managerial success

A child miseducated is a child lost.

(John F Kennedy)

If you want children to keep their feet on the ground,
put some responsibility on their shoulders.

(A Van Buren)

Give a man a fish, and you feed him for a day;
teach a man to fish, and you feed him for a lifetime.

(Chinese proverb)

A long time ago, a 52-year-old man was taking his youngest son to the airport. As they were bidding each other farewell, the father said:

Son, I am like a candle that burned throughout the years in order to shed light for you, for your brothers and sisters, and for the whole family. Now that you are off to study in the United States, you must light your own candle, for yourself now and for your own children in the future.

As the 17-year-old son left his country, his thoughts lingered, *"I wonder what my father was mumbling about . . . candles and light."* It didn't take long, however, before the young man started realizing the significance of what his father meant on that day in the departure lounge . . . for indeed he was completely on his own upon arrival to the new country, alone for the first time in a strange land. He had to light his own candle in order to survive, and as the years went by, he became much more aware that the candle he had lit was sturdy, durable and well made. Unknown to him, his father had been helping him construct that candle, patiently and lovingly, directly and indirectly, throughout his childhood and adolescence.

Here is how I, the young man back then, remember my father:

- He was a great coach and mentor.
- He gave my brothers and me early responsibility: working summers and vacations in his housing construction business while we were in high school.
- He provided guidance and advice when we were solving our problems, learning from our mistakes, and making tough decisions – in brief, he taught us how to "fish".
- He was an excellent role model: a self-made man; a hard worker; a great example of honesty and integrity in his business dealings.
- Finally, he knew how to balance love, discipline and fun.

Slowly but surely he was helping us construct our own candles.

I made sure to pass my father's wisdom to our three children, slowly and patiently helping them make their own candles. I pray that they, too, will pass their grandfather's legacy to their own children.

This chapter is dedicated to helping others construct strong and durable candles, for themselves and for their young children. The emphasis, however, will be more on developing people in management, by uncovering the common characteristics and ingredients that pave the road to success in organizational leadership and management. This chapter will also highlight the research implications for both child upbringing and recruitment. Although it is based mainly on a study of the education and development of Gulf executives, it draws heavily from other international research on the ingredients for managerial success.

The findings of this research, completed in 1989 and updated in 2002, were guided by the concepts shown in Figure 1.1.

Managerial success requires certain competencies defined here as skills, knowledge and attitude. Some of these competencies

Ingredients for success → **Competencies** → **Managerial success**
Ten Ingredients:

The first five

• Quality of education	Skills	Accomplishments
• Exposure & role models	Knowledge	and contributions
• Early responsibility	Attitudes	(observable and
• Ethics and values		sometimes
• Self-development		measurable)

The second five
- Training opportunities
- Standards and feedback
- The knowledge base
- Formal career development
- A problem-solving culture

Figure 1.1 Ingredients and competencies for managerial success

are learned through training (on and off the job) and work experience. Other competencies, perhaps the more important, are learned early in life and are anchored in values, beliefs and attitudes.

Managerial competencies have been extensively researched and are now fairly well known. See, for example, the American Management Association's (AMA) research in the early 1980s summarized in *The Competent Manager* (Boyatzis, 1982); David McClelland's early research (described in Spencer and Spencer, 1993); followed by the writings on emotional intelligence (Daniel Goleman, 1995, 1998); and most recently the emphasis on talent (Buckingham and Coffman, 1999, and Buckingham and Clifton, 2001). Chapter 2 of this book, covers in more detail the subject of managerial competencies.

In the 1989 Meirc study, 140 Arab Gulf managers were identified by over 50 organizations as notably successful, and each was interviewed at length in order to find out when, how and where they acquired their competencies. In 2002, another sample of 181 Arab executives and managers were asked to rank order the same ingredients for success, and add to them others from their own experience. (For the 2002 results, and for the interview schedules and questionnaire used in the two studies, see Appendix at the end of this book).

Our research looked into *when, how* and *where* managers acquire or learn these managerial competencies. The results were fascinating, partly because what was discovered is probably true of successful managers in any culture. Far more important, however, is that most of the successful executives acquired their managerial competencies well before starting their careers. Child upbringing and education were cited as the primary sources for learning the competencies required for success in management; competencies, which are, it seems, learned by one's early to mid-twenties.

The ingredients for managerial success

The key findings of our research were the ten ingredients of success identified by the managers we interviewed. Not all ten ingredients were present for every manager, but it was clear that the more of these ten factors a person possesses or exhibits, the greater his or her chances of becoming successful. The first five ingredients were:

1 quality of education
2 exposure and role models
3 early responsibility
4 ethics and values
5 self-development.

These first five ingredients were basically the result of child upbringing, interaction with family members, peers, teachers and others; all acquired well before the future manager reached the workplace. The second five ingredients occurred during the manager's career, and will be covered in Chapter 2.

Quality of education

The quality of education refers not as much to the individual's academic qualifications, as to the experience and excellence of education received: the stretching of the mind, learning to think, interacting with high caliber students and teachers, participating in extra-curricular activities and events, and the encounter with new worlds and new people. This experience starts at kindergarten and school, and becomes more prominent and valuable at university. It is a critical ingredient to building a strong and well-constructed candle.

Wise teachers and parents realize that a great number of managerial competencies are learned during the crucial early years while a person is a student: social and emotional skills such as achievement drive, teamwork, leadership, followership, accountability and self-dependence, negotiation and communication skills, and, last but not least, analytical thinking. My wife and I made it a point to continually encourage our daughters to be highly involved in all sorts of school events, sports, drama and music, and other extra-curricular activities, even sometimes at the expense of getting the highest grades. It is through these activities that children gain the skills and competencies needed for becoming successful managers and leaders.

Here is how two executives described their experiences as university students:

> *Being active in the Student Association at the university (in the USA), I developed a talent for debate and communication.*

> *At that time I was the only foreign student at the college (in the UK) . . . this was a challenge . . . an unforgettable experience.*

Often, though, most parents I speak with are deeply concerned, even worried, about their children's grades, especially when the school's main emphasis is on rote learning as well as passing exams. As in many parts of the world, and particularly in the Middle East, there is a serious annual crisis called the "final exams" period where one or both parents start cramming data and information into their children's heads just prior to the examinations. The effectiveness of this last-minute filling of the knowledge gap produced by the educational institutions is debatable. And how valuable or useful this rote learning is for life's future challenges is even more questionable.

Rote learning and memorizing, which are characteristic features of many educational systems in the Arab world, need to be replaced by a more experiential approach to learning, together with increased emphasis on extra-curricular activities, project work, sports, and so on. In addition, creative thinking and learning skills rather than memorizing and copying should be encouraged, recognized and rewarded.

> *I hear and I forget,*
> *I see and I remember,*
> *I do and I understand.*
> (Confucius)

Since educational systems, in general, take quite a while to change for the better, it becomes incumbent on teachers and parents to exert the extra effort in order to encourage experiential learning and extra-curricular activities, rather than adding more water to the mud. Of course, good grades (along with high scores on standardized tests, such as the Scholastic Aptitude Test (SAT)) are important for future admission to good universities; but most excellent universities also look closely at the student's extra-curricular accomplishments for admission decisions. This is increasingly being done through personal interviews with the applicants to evaluate personality and the above-mentioned accomplishments prior to admitting students.

Even later on in life, most good employers will give equal, if not more, weight to analytical thinking and interpersonal skills as compared to high grades when recruiting graduates. Ask yourself which of these two candidates you would hire for a future managerial job: the first graduate with outstanding grades (say, with a Grade Point Average (GPA) of 3.95 out of 4.00) who spent most of his or her university years going from home to class to the library, or the second graduate with a 2.90 average who was active in sports, debating clubs, student associations, and so on. And what if this second graduate had to earn some of the tuition by working during the semesters? The choice for me is fairly easy, especially if both candidates graduated from the same university with the same major.

Finally, recent research on emotional intelligence (EI) suggests that cognitive abilities alone are not sufficient for success in personal and organizational effectiveness (cognitive abilities like language fluency, logic, and abstract reasoning normally use only the analytical functions and areas of the human brain). Emotional competence, such as self-awareness, self-management, social awareness and relationship management, are equally, if not more, essential for success (Goleman, 1998). The implications for educational institutions are clear: schools and universities have to incorporate into their curricula and extra-curricular activities proper training specifically focused on social and emotional skills. Here is what Goleman, one of the pioneers on the subject of emotional intelligence, had to say:

> *Given our new understanding of the crucial role emotional competence plays in individual, group, and organizational success, the implications for education are clear: We should be helping young people master these competencies as essential life skills. There are already numerous school-based programs in the basics of EI, programs that deliver social and emotional learning (SEL).*

Goleman goes on to say:

> *Given that employers themselves are looking for EI capacities in those they hire, colleges and professional schools that offered appropriate SEL training would benefit both their graduates and the organizations they work for. The most forward-looking educators will, I hope, recognize the importance of emotional*

intelligence in higher education, not just for the students, not just for the student's employers, but for the vitality of an economy – and society – as a whole. As Erasmus, the great humanist writer, tells us, "The best hope of a nation lies in the proper education of its youth."

(Cherniss and Goleman, 2001)

Exposure and role models

This second ingredient refers to the idea of learning from others through exposure and role models.

Continuous exposure to and interaction with other people and cultures widens the horizon of the young, and gives them opportunities to learn alternative ways of thinking and living. Travel, in and out of one's country, is an opportunity to learn from others and ought to become an integral part of school and home education. I have seen too many families who visit London, Cairo, Athens or New York without ever taking their children to museums or other intellectual and cultural treasures of these cities. Shopping areas and amusement parks are not the only places to spend one's vacation!

Furthermore, exposure to others and learning from them is a continuous process, not only for the young. It is a life-long method of learning and developing skills. Even nations and organizations learn from each other; for example, we have witnessed how Japanese businessmen learned from others for decades. And excellent organizations continue to benchmark best business practices with a view to learning and improving. Indeed, if other societies, companies or people have found an efficient solution to a problem, then learning from them can save both resources and effort.

One of the Omani executives we interviewed described the benefits she derived from being an expatriate:

The cross-posting to Malaysia broadened my outlook and increased confidence in myself . . . I learned from the Malaysian nationals as well as the Western expatriates . . . . From this experience, I now know how expats think of nationals; being an expat myself, I appreciate the feelings of expats we have here; and I proved myself outside my own country thus removing any doubts about being promoted just because I am a national.

Equally important are the role models in one's life. Parents, relatives, friends or teachers are often the main role models we know. They shape us more than we think. They are the people (the significant others) whom we respect, admire, aspire to emulate, or wish to please. They are the persons (deceased or living) who have exerted great influence on our values and beliefs, which ultimately and indirectly influenced our managerial competencies.

An executive remembering his role model, his father:

He taught me to never fear problems . . . "for every problem there is a solution" he always said. Once, his ship (loaded with merchandise) sank off the coast. He came back swimming and later told me "the lost ship is history . . . think ahead now".

We need role models throughout life to inspire us, to encourage us to excel, and to give us the inner power and comfort we need for success now or in the future, sometimes long after our role models are gone. I have had three role models in my life, so far. The first, my father, had a tremendous influence on me when it came to ethics and values, and especially so when it came to integrity.

My other two role models were my first manager and my father-in-law. One exerted his influence when I was in my mid-twenties and the other during my early thirties. The former taught me the value of on-the-job training and coaching, and the latter the value of quality and continuous learning. This is how each went about it.

When I started my career with a manufacturing company, the Financial Controller in one of its plants in California took me and another MBA graduate under his wing. As our coach, he would take the time to patiently explain the value of learning the nitty-gritty of every job in the Finance department, reminding us that we couldn't be effective managers if we did not know the jobs of our future employees. We mastered all the accounting functions, including taking inventories of work in process and finished goods. And when we were hit by the MBA "blues", he would listen to us with understanding, kindness and empathy, raising our morale and motivating us to complete our training program. He was an excellent coach.

The third role model was my father-in-law, the founder of Meirc. Shortly after joining Meirc when I was in my early-thirties, it became clear that his mentoring skills were superior. He guided and counseled me during the many and lengthy conversations on the subject of career development, including my own. It was partly his influence which made me decide to change careers from finance to human resources. Above all, he really drove home the value of quality in our profession as trainers and consultants, and the importance of continuous learning throughout life – "from the cradle to the grave" – as he so often quoted. His support was crucial when I returned to university for the doctorate program after nearly ten years of employment. He was a great mentor.

Early responsibility

Early responsibility is the third ingredient, a factor that has been frequently cited by writers as a major contributor to future managerial success (see AMA's report by Margerison and Kakabadse, 1984; Cox and Cooper (1988) on high flyers; Kotter, 1990, and Bennis, 1989, to name only a few). This refers not so much to work-related responsibility but to responsibility at home, in the family and often in a family business early on in life. A child or a teenager who, either out of necessity or as a deliberate part of his or her upbringing, is given small jobs or has to work for a living will acquire at an early age the self-confidence, the ability to make decisions and the sense of accountability which some people otherwise learn too late in life.

Charles Handy, our adviser during the Meirc research, summarized the ten ingredients of success in a concise chapter entitled "Teach Your Children Well" (*Beyond Certainty*, 1996). On early responsibility, he wrote:

> *Entrepreneurs in this country [the UK] often come from impoverished backgrounds, or have been forced into early responsibility by the death of a parent. The most successful expatriates, another study revealed, are those who have had the most disruption in their youth, and have survived. It is dangerous, it seems, to make life too comfortable for one's young.*

Early responsibility, I believe, was the main ingredient used by my father in building the candles of his children. One manager we interviewed described early responsibility as the "business school of life". His father, a wealthy businessman, put him to work every summer vacation along with construction workers and operators. The young son hated every moment of those long, sizzling Kuwaiti summers; but when I interviewed him many years later he looked back with nostalgia on those summers and said: "I learned so much during those days ... perhaps as much as I've learned from my business degree". It is easy to guess who this manager's role model was.

Children too can be given small responsibilities: from tidying up their rooms, to washing the family car, to all sorts of other help around the house. Earning some pocket money while in school and university is certainly a valuable experience. Early responsibility prepares people for life, and as the Chinese proverb goes, it is like teaching people how to fish, instead of feeding them a fish every day. All three of our daughters were encouraged to work during their high school and university years. Although the pay was meager, the experience was invaluable.

Most of the managers in the AMA study (Margerison and Kakabadse, 1984), as well as the managers we talked to, felt that early responsibility must come before the age of 30 and preferably before the age of 25.

Ethics and values

The fourth ingredient refers to the work ethic, the code of behavior, which induces hard and honest work. This is the belief that quality and excellence are important by themselves, that if a job is worth doing it is worth doing well, and that integrity, respect for time and commitment to work count for something. Individuals with high standards of ethics and values are usually self-motivated – they don't have to be pushed – they push themselves. They are highly achievement-oriented – they derive great satisfaction from reaching their goals and ambitions.

A Bahraini manager describing his work ethic:

> ... I come from a hard working family. Although my parents are illiterate, all their children are well educated and have responsible jobs: ... I wish I could slow down my pace of work, but I've been doing this [working hard] since childhood ... I want to be the best in what I do.

Ethics and values are often learned from religious and cultural teachings. They are also learned by observing the behavior of admired ones, and through discussions and conversations with parents, relatives, friends and teachers. They can be internalized either early in life or at later stages. Role models, too, can be particularly influential, as we noted earlier.

Jack Welch, former Chairman and CEO of General Electric, described in the first chapter of his book (*Jack: Straight from the Gut*, 2001) the great influence his parents had on his ethics and values. Here is what he said about his mother's influence:

> *And many of my basic management beliefs – things like competing hard to win, facing reality, motivating people by alternately hugging and kicking them, setting stretch goals, and relentlessly following up on people to make sure things get done – can be traced to her as well. The insights she drilled into me never faded . . . . Perhaps the greatest single gift she gave me was self-confidence.*

Welch ends his book with a description of his GE retirement party in 2001 with these words: "It was some night. I wish my mother could have been there".

Another factor, which was frequently mentioned by many of the successful executives we interviewed, was the importance of motivation, mainly self-motivation. A great deal of thought and research went into the subject of motivation, from the ancient Greeks to the twentieth-century writers such as Maslow, McClelland, Skinner, Herzberg, Vroom and so many more. Perhaps the thinking about motivation which I like most can be summarized by what John Adair calls the "Fifty-Fifty Principle": "Fifty per cent of motivation comes from within a person and fifty per cent from his or her environment, especially from the leadership encountered there", (Adair, 1996). The more difficult question, however, is how much of that first fifty per cent is influenced by child upbringing. I suspect that most of that fifty is closely related to our first five ingredients. The elements that make up the second fifty per cent will be discussed in Chapter 3.

Self-development

The fifth ingredient is manifested by a burning desire, an insatiable thirst, a passion for continuous learning throughout life; an acknowledgement and a desire for self-improvement and development. Again, I believe, this phenomenon starts at birth. Parents and teachers can continuously encourage the young to read, discuss, analyze, and have an inquisitive mind.

Parents, for example, could make a valuable habit of giving their children books, magazines, educational software and toys – along with the other play toys. However, parents must also take the next necessary step: follow up with the child by discussing the book or sharing the educational toy. In short, they must ensure that the child is actually internalizing the habit of continuous learning. Of course, it is futile simply to tell the child to read books while the parent is never seen doing the same. It is like telling the child not to smoke while the parent is constantly lighting up! Lead by example, and "walk the talk", as managers are always advised to do.

Perhaps a personal experience can best summarize my view on self-development. A short time after I completed my doctorate degree at the age of 36, my wife and I were wondering whether it was all worth it. Was it worth spending our savings, sacrificing almost four years of good earnings, and landing in debt just to get the higher degree? "Yes, I believe it was worth it", I said. Then she asked this sobering question: "What was the one most significant thing you learned during those four years?" After a few moments of deep thought, I replied, "I learned how little I now know, and how much more there is to learn".

We recall I am sure, how some of us felt upon graduation from high school: we believed that we had learned everything there was to learn! However, let us always remember that regardless of how much we know, it is never enough. Life challenges us to excel at being both enthusiastic students and inspiring teachers.

In summary, a child's upbringing and development seems to be the base and foundation for managerial development. Education builds on that foundation. And when we start our business career, most excellent organizations offer golden training opportunities to build further on what we have learned during childhood and during our academic years. See Figure 1.2.

Parents as well as organizations can use the first five ingredients to supplement or enhance their existing practices of child development and recruitment respectively. After discussing the research findings, my wife and I were encouraged to implement several new child rearing ideas (some appear below). Several organizations used the research findings when recruiting fresh

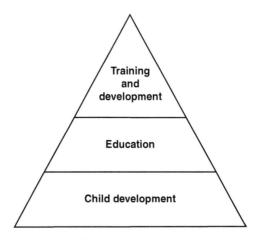

Figure 1.2 Upbringing and development

university graduates, especially during the initial screening interviews.

> *If child development is so crucial to the development of successful managers, then more attention ought to be given to it by parents, instead of relegating this responsibility to teachers, or nannies or maids. Child development is the foundation for management development – good results cannot be expected from training and management development if the basic foundation is weak.*
>
> *(The Making of Gulf Managers,* Meiric Training & Consulting, 1989)

We will start with a brief checklist for parents, followed later by one for recruiters.

Brief checklist for parents

The first five ingredients are listed below:

Quality of education

- extra-curricular activities: sports, drama, art, music, debating clubs, student associations, and school events
- school trips to cultural/historical places or trips to foreign countries
- research papers and projects, not rote learning
- emphasis on analytical thinking and learning how to think, not merely passing examinations
- reading or studying subjects outside one's specialization or major
- part-time or summer work.

Exposure and role models

- visits to historical and cultural sites when traveling overseas;
- learning from expatriates working in the country or from foreign students and tourists
- watching news and documentaries (for example, science, history and geography), along with other TV programs
- reading biographies, autobiographies, literature, and history books
- be a good role model to your children
- identify role models and mentors throughout life; seek their advice and counsel.

Early responsibility

- small tasks or chores given to children, ranging from cleaning their room to washing the family car
- part-time jobs and summer employment
- volunteer work for charitable or community organizations
- participation in certain family decisions or in planning family events
- teach them at a young age to plan and organize their own activities
- preparation of own budget and keeping account of main expenses during high school and university
- insist on accountability, but allow learning from mistakes.

Ethics and values

- teach by example: integrity, honesty, and hard work
- importance of excellence and quality: "if a job is worth doing, it is worth doing well"
- pride in achievement and the importance of having a mission in life

- teach them to respect and value time
- the value of perseverance and endurance necessary to accomplish a task
- the importance of self-respect, self-awareness, and self-confidence, balanced with respect for others.

Self-development

- set a good example by actions which demonstrate an inquiring mind, a desire to learn, and the willingness to go out and search for knowledge/experience
- actively encourage continuous self-learning through listening, thinking and reading
- encourage creativity and critical thinking
- give educational materials as gifts/presents (books, software, toys, etc.)
- subscriptions to journals and magazines
- educational television and websites, balanced with other entertainment programs/sites
- attending seminars, speaking events and discussion groups.

Brief checklist for recruiters

Recruiters will do well to use these five ingredients during initial screening of candidates, especially young graduates who lack previous work experience. During the probing and the process of "uncovering the mask", questions from *each* of the ingredients can be posed to applicants. Here are sample questions for each ingredient:

Quality of education

- What extra-curricular activities did you participate in? In what role? What did you learn from the experience? Name some specific skills learned during that experience.
- How would you apply a specific theory or body of knowledge (fill in the blank) to practical day-to-day life situations? Examples: How would you use your knowledge of group dynamics in building teams that are more effective? Or, what problems is a company likely to encounter when launching a new product? Followed by: How would you overcome such problems?
- What projects or research did you carry out? Was it individual or group work? If group, what problems did you face and how were they resolved?
- How did you spend your time during summer vacations and holidays?
- Who is the one most memorable person (or event) that affected you during your university years? Followed by how and why?

Exposure and role models

- During your travels overseas (if any, during college or holidays), what impressed you most? Why?
- Have you interacted with any foreign students at school or university? If yes, what would you say were the most important benefits derived from the encounters?
- Who are the people in your life that you respect, admire or aspire to emulate (role models)? Why is (or was) this person your role model? Describe their influence on you. What specifically was learned from a particular role model?

Early responsibility

- Describe specific instances or situations when responsibility was assumed by you. Why, where and when did these events occur? How did you handle them? Were they voluntary or forced upon you by circumstances?
- Describe a success and/or a failure when assuming a certain responsibility. Followed by deeper probing questions.
- If the application form/letter shows some work experience, ask applicant to describe how it was handled and what was learned.

Ethics and values

- Describe one or two achievements that you are particularly proud of. What specific efforts, skills or attitudes were required to accomplish these achievements?
- What motivated you to overcome the obstacles, if any, and to get the job done?
- If you were given a very hard and difficult task to do with limited time, how would you go about doing it? Why did you choose your solution?
- What do you want out of life? Followed by several probing questions to ensure that the answers are genuine.
- If you were to inherit fifty million dollars, what would you do? Followed by more probing questions.

Note that this ingredient is probably the most difficult one to assess and probe. It involves a set of beliefs. Therefore, questions must revolve around certain past actions or behavior that demonstrate honesty, integrity, hard work, quality, orientation toward achievement, and self-motivation.

Self-development

- What book or article have you read recently? Please tell me something about it.
- Can you recall an interesting conversation you had recently with another person? What was it about? Followed by: What did you learn as a result of it?
- What TV programs do you watch most? What are your favorite web sites, or what do you use the Internet for?
- Do you belong to a book club or have you recently attended an educational event?
- Which book, journal or magazine have you recently bought or subscribed to? Ask the candidate to tell you more about it.

These and many other questions should be tailored to suit the educational background and circumstances of the interviewee, and the interviewing style of the recruiter. The examples of questions presented above are merely guidelines, and should certainly be asked in a fuller, more personalized and natural manner.

Chapter Two

The iceberg

Competencies and human resources management

If you wish to plan for a year, sow seeds,
If you wish to plan for ten years, plant trees,
If you wish to plan for a lifetime, develop people.
(Kuan Chung Tzu, 7th century BC)

One swallow does not make spring.
(Aristotle)

In a hierarchy every employee tends to rise to his level of incompetence.
(Laurence J Peter, *The Peter Principle*)

Competitors can easily, and legitimately, copy most products and business practices in relatively short periods. For instance, it does not take too long to imitate a new banking or insurance product, or an innovative marketing campaign. It may take a little bit longer though to copy a new consumer or industrial product, especially when patented. People in your organization, however, are much more difficult to copy. It is nearly impossible to copy their mindset, motivation, and their attitudes; in short, the competencies of your human capital.

In this chapter, we will first describe how competencies are used in the field of human resources management (HRM). Later, we will re-visit the ten ingredients for success, five of which were discussed in Chapter 1. These ingredients represent the how, when and where managers acquire their competencies.

What is a competency?

Competency-based human resources management has become the newest fad. Recruitment, performance management, compensation, training, career development, and so forth, have all become competency based. What is a competency anyway? Why the recent enthusiasm about competencies?

There are almost as many definitions of competence and competency as there are books on the subject. The Oxford English Dictionary defines competency as "a skill you need in a particular job or for a particular task". And according to Webster's Dictionary, competence is the "possession of required skill, knowledge, qualification, or capacity; having suitable or sufficient skill, knowledge, experience, etc. for some purpose".

Scott Parry (1997 and 2000) defined competency as "a cluster of related knowledge, skills and attitudes working together to produce outstanding performance in a given area of responsibility".

It seems that there is widespread agreement that a competency is a combination of three elements: *Skills*, *Knowledge*, and *Attitudes* (SKA). However, it should be quickly noted that there is disagreement on what constitutes the third element;

some refer to it as attitudes (as we shall do in this chapter), others use any one of the following terms: enduring character-istics, personal attributes, emotional intelligence, or talent.

In order to simplify and enhance our understanding of competencies, I chose the metaphor of the iceberg, which has been used previously by other writers. The competency iceberg is made of all three elements: skills, knowledge and attitude.

It is well known that around seven eighths of an iceberg is below water, leaving around 12 per cent representing the proverbial "tip of the iceberg". However, did you know that the glacial ice that icebergs are made of might be around 16,000 years old! Every year more snow and ice are deposited on the glacial ice until a large piece breaks away (calves) and becomes a floating iceberg. It was such an iceberg that sank the *Titanic* in 1912.

The tip of the iceberg represents the *skills* (S). These are the capabilities and the technical know-how, the "how-to", and the "what" needed to get the job done efficiently. Fixing or operating a car or a machine, using a computer or a spreadsheet, giving a safe hypodermic injection – these are skills that can be learned and acquired through practice and experience.

Around the water level is *knowledge* (K), which is gained through education (theory), and by experience (practice). Accountants know the rules of double entry bookkeeping; engineers know the principles of thermo-dynamics, and so forth. They also know why "things" work the way they do.

The combination of skills (S) and knowledge (K) are considered a person's expertise – the "*what* is required" to do the job. Expertise is a baseline competence you need to get the job done, but it is *how* you do the job that determines superior performance. This is where attitude becomes a very significant factor.

Below the water surface are *attitudes* (A), making up the largest part of the iceberg. Attitudes and subsequent behavior are part and parcel of recurring and enduring patterns of thinking, feelings, motives, beliefs and values. Attitudes influence "how" a person behaves, and "why" a person behaves in a certain way. *Attitudes shape how the job is done.*

To illustrate the concept of competencies during our seminars, I often use these simple examples: You come across a taxi driver who is taking you to the airport; he is a skilled driver (S), he knows the traffic rules well and even the mechanical aspects of the car (K), but his driving style is at best reckless, he is keeping you on edge, and is often hazardous to other drivers (A). Would you hire him to work for your organization? What if you have a member of your team who is a genius at his specialization, but cannot get along with his fellow team members; or worse yet, he gets things done while walking all over his colleagues? What if you have a departmental manager, who runs an efficient operation, yet is constantly stabbing other department heads in the back? Clearly, the highest skills and the best knowledge alone are not sufficient for superior performance. It is attitudes that distinguish superior performers from others.

Why the recent enthusiasm?

Competency studies have been around for many years. They have been used extensively by the military since World War II. Competency-based methods have also been used in education and in health care for some time. In the 1970s, Professor David McClelland of Harvard University and a group of researchers started investigating the competencies required for superior job performance. In his paper "Testing for Competence Rather than Intelligence", McClelland (1973) stated that academic aptitude, school grades, and advanced degrees simply did not predict how well people would perform on the job, or even whether they would succeed in life. Instead, he proposed that a set of specific competencies such as empathy, self-discipline, and initiative distinguished the most successful from those who were just good enough to keep their jobs.

From the 1980s onward, other management writers took up McClelland's work. For example, Richard Boyatzis summarized an American Management Association (AMA) study in his book *The Competent Manager* (1982), in which he identified 18 managerial competencies. The 1990s saw a number of books on competencies, for example, Spencer and Spencer (1993), and the two books by Goleman (1995 and 1998), where he examined 25 emotional intelligence competencies.

In their recent book, *Primal Leadership* (2002), Goleman, Boyatzis and McKee listed 18 leadership competencies under four categories:

- *Self-awareness*: emotional self-awareness, accurate self-assessment, and self-confidence
- *Self-management*: self-control, transparency, adaptability, achievement, initiative, and optimism
- *Social awareness*: empathy, organizational awareness, and service
- *Relationship management*: inspiration, influence, developing others, change catalyst, teamwork and collaboration, and conflict management.

Everyone, it seems, has joined the bandwagon; here are a few titles published in the past decade focused on competencies in the work place:

- *Management: A Competency Approach* (2001).
- *The Complete Guide to Training Delivery: A Competency-Based Approach* (2000).

- *Competency-Based Recruitment and Selection* (1998).
- *Core Competency-Based Strategy* (1997).
- *Competency-Based Performance Improvement: A Strategy for Organizational Change* (1993).

In addition, a quick search on the Internet would show hundreds of websites that advertise competency models, toolkits, and packages.

So, why the recent interest in competencies, even though we have been aware of their importance for many years? Here is my conjecture: with the escalation of competition in global trade and the start of the information revolution, quality of products and services – as well as market-creating innovations – became essential for business survival. American and European corporations went on the offensive in the 1980s in order to slow down and eventually reverse the Asian, especially Japanese, penetration of world markets. Witness the rise of Canon in the copying and imaging fields, Honda and Toyota in car manufacturing, Sony in multimedia and network solutions; and the list goes on and on.

However, creating new competitive advantages in innovative products, quality or service required new managerial thinking and behavior. There was a need to introduce change and continuous improvement, implement new global strategies, encourage technical innovations, make substantial capital investments, and adopt leaner structures and faster response time, among many others. Consequently, human capital moved to the forefront in strategy formulation. Achieving new competitive advantages now meant having "competent" employees, colleagues, associates who possess more than just superior skills and knowledge. They had to have certain competencies (enduring characteristics, talents, and attitudes) such as: excellence at teamwork, leadership, quality mindset, creativity, initiative and resourcefulness, empathy, adaptability, visionary and strategic thinking, market-orientation, a passion for serving the customer, and so forth. All of these competencies are found deep in the core of the iceberg, well below the surface of the water.

> *The rules for work are changing. We're being judged by a new yardstick: not just by how smart we are, or by our training and experience, but also by how well we handle ourselves and each other. This yardstick is increasingly applied in choosing who will be hired and who will not, who will be let go and who will be retained, who passed over and who promoted.*
>
> (Daniel Goleman, *Working with Emotional Intelligence*, 1998)

Competency-based HRM

Competency-based HRM simply means that skills, knowledge and attitudes (the SKAs), once determined for a specific organization, are incorporated into recruitment practices, performance appraisals, compensation, promotion decisions, training, and career development activities.

There are many approaches for determining the SKAs. Some organizations identify core competencies expected of all employees. Others define specific competencies for each job description, which I call professional competencies. More comprehensive competency models go further by defining levels of competence within each job category. It will not be possible to review in depth these various approaches in one chapter. Instead, I will present a very brief description of methods used to determine competencies. This short description will cover: (1) core competencies for managerial level or critical jobs; (2) professional competencies that are specific for each job or profession; and (3) examples of levels of competence within job categories.

Starting with its statement of vision, mission or purpose, an organization derives a set of *core competencies* that all individuals in critical or managerial jobs are expected to acquire or improve. Additionally, the vision and strategy formulation exercise would normally yield a number of competitive advantages as well as a set of corporate values. For instance, if one of the competitive advantages were the quality of customer service, then one of the core competencies would be customer-orientation. If one of the corporate values were innovation, then another core competency would be creative thinking, and so forth. Such core competencies define what that particular organization values most in its people. Core competencies are the behavioral aspects that differentiate superior performers from the average ones, and they would include mostly attitudes, with less emphasis on skills and knowledge.

Professional competencies, on the other hand, are related to specific professions or jobs. Given that they are job-specific, these competencies (SKAs) will normally concentrate more on skills and knowledge items and less on attitudes. For example, a bank teller would have a different set of SKAs than an accountant; one handles cash and the other constructs financial statements. Likewise, a marketing manager requires a different set of competencies than a production supervisor. Each job or specialization would have its own set of skills and knowledge with a few attitudinal items.

Core and professional competencies are both further differentiated by degrees of difficulty and complexity according to the level of the job. For example, a junior technician or a junior buyer would require basic knowledge (BK) and skills, while a senior technician or a senior buyer is expected to be fully competent (FC) on the very same item or task. Similarly, a section manager would be required to lead a small number of supervisors and get them to work as a team, while the Chief Executive Officer (CEO) is required to do the same for the whole organization.

At this point, three examples are sufficient to illustrate the idea of competency levels.

Professional competency

Example 1
Technician: Knowledge of electronic and electrical fields, such as: RF communication principles, electrical waves, microelectronics, electrical theory, and fiber optics and laser technology.

Level: Basic knowledge   Working knowledge   Fully competent
              (BK)   (WK)   (FC)

Example 2
Buyer: Preparation of purchasing plans and negotiation strategy for supply chain management based on analysis of relevant data and information on suppliers, competitors, and markets.

Level: Basic knowledge   Working knowledge   Fully competent
              (BK)   (WK)   (FC)

Core competency: "Helicopter view" or "Clarity of purpose".

Example 3
It is defined as "understanding the entirety of a business situation and seeing clearly what needs to be done, and how to accomplish it".

This same core competency is required at all five (hypothetical) managerial levels. This is how it is further defined for two different levels:

Level 1 (Junior Manager)
- sees the whole picture and identifies departmental goals and targets
- clearly understands what needs to be done to accomplish a goal
- prioritizes items in order of importance
- clearly distinguishes between what is important and what is urgent.

Level 5 (President or CEO)
- develops strategic plans that significantly impact the business
- ensures that there is integration and clarity in complex business plans
- specifies the steps required to be taken by the organization to be successful
- anticipates the effect of changes in the external environment, and takes appropriate actions.

How are competencies measured? This is the most frequently asked question, and perhaps the most contentious, and the hardest to answer.

Professional competencies are measured by the demonstrated capability of a person to perform a job at a certain level of expertise. Establishing the level of capabilities can be done by asking a series of questions such as these: Can the person describe or discuss the tasks required to do a certain job (BK)? Do they know the principles (BK)? Is the job holder able to do the tasks well (WK)? Can the person solve unanticipated problems related to the tasks (WK)? Are they able to train others on the tasks (FC)? Are they capable of improving or introducing changes to current practices (FC)? Are they called upon to provide advice on their area of specialization (FC)? A taskforce of line supervisors/managers and HR specialists should be formed to agree on the definitions of levels (BK, WK, and FC), and the questions to be asked in order to determine the levels of competence for professional jobs.

Core competencies are even harder to measure since they are more subjective and soft in nature. For instance, how does one measure "market-orientation" or "creativity"? The best answer is this: core competencies are measured by observable behavior over a period of time. How frequently does the sales representative or the sales manager get together with customers and how good is the relationship? In the case of creative thinking, one would ask how often and how well did a person generate new ideas? Invariably, I recommend to participants attending our seminars to keep a record of their actions or accomplishments in order to be able to demonstrate the "observable behavior criteria" required by a certain competency. I also share with them this interesting anecdote in order to stress the significance of the *frequency* of observable behavior.

San Juan Capistrano is a small coastal town in southern California famous for its "legend of the swallows". The swallows are small birds that migrate every year from Argentina, 12,000 km away, to California. Their northward migration takes them to Capistrano where they spend the summer to raise their young. In the winter the swallows return to Argentina. I share this famous saying by Aristotle with seminar participants: "*One swallow does not make spring*". One needs to see a whole flock of swallows before one is certain that spring has arrived! One or two visits with customers a year do not demonstrate market-orientation. Likewise, one creative idea a year does not indicate a competency for creative thinking.

At the organizational and departmental levels, the desired outcomes of core competencies are perhaps easier to measure. For instance, if customer service is a core competency, which is linked to the overall strategy and success of an organization, data are collected in order to measure customer service. For example, a hotel may examine the results of a mystery shopper/guest research; or one can look closely at records of complaints and customer satisfaction surveys; or analyze the data on repeat customers and occupancy rates. There are many key performance indicators (KPIs) that are used to measure the strength of organizational-level core competencies, such as new products for innovation, or accident rates for safety, and so on.

Once core and professional competencies are identified, they can be used for various HR functions. To be more specific:

- Competencies are used in recruitment and selection where interviewers and decision makers can check candidates for the desired SKAs.
- Core competencies can be incorporated into the performance management process.
- Gaps in knowledge and skills are identified and translated into training and career development plans.
- Competencies are utilized in coaching and mentoring programs.
- Core competencies are also used for identifying high potential employees, or the high flyers as some organizations call them. These people are identified as high flyers for the purposes of compensation, promotion, career development, or succession planning.

> *Having a skill gap does not mean someone is a poor performer. If we are to grow as a business, everyone will have skill gaps at one time or another. However, not taking action to fill a gap, once it has been identified, is poor performance and will be assessed as such.*
>
> (A Managing Director, Shell)

One final observation about the competency iceberg, skills (S) and knowledge (K) are relatively *easy* to acquire through education, training and developmental activities. Attitudes (A), however, are more *difficult* to develop or change.

Attitudes, as we saw earlier, relate to beliefs, values and motives – these are learned early in life. They are the products of child upbringing and education. It seems, then, that the first 16 or 18 years of life are crucial to the formation of the largest, and perhaps most important, part of the competency iceberg. It is interesting to note again that an iceberg breaks off from glacial ice, which was formed over a period of 16,000 years!

Re-visiting the ingredients for managerial success

In Chapter 1, The candle, we presented the Meirc research findings (1989 and updated in 2002) in which managers we interviewed identified ten ingredients for managerial success. We asked the managers *how, when* and *where* they developed their competencies. We also asked probing open-ended questions to find what factors, events, or people contributed to their success. In brief, how did they get to their present senior positions? The results were fascinating and rather surprising since the first five ingredients occurred *well before* the managers started their careers. Indeed, competencies were learned and developed mostly during childhood and adolescence as the result of interaction with parents, family members, peers, and teachers throughout the years of formal education. Interestingly enough, these competencies stem from beliefs, values and motives, which later in life will shape attitudes and behavior.

The next five ingredients for success were more or less initiated, managed, and controlled by managers or by the organization, as we shall see shortly.

The ten ingredients for managerial success

The first five ingredients (covered in Chapter 1, The candle) are:

1 Quality of education
2 Exposure and role models
3 Early responsibility
4 Ethics and values
5 Self-development

The second five ingredients are:

6 *Training opportunities*
7 *Standards and feedback*
8 *The knowledge base*
9 *Formal career development*
10 *A problem-solving culture*

Training opportunities

By training opportunities we mean the provision of formal internal and external training programs as well as structured on-the-job training. Of course, the benefits of training programs and workshops are not only restricted to the acquisition of skills and knowledge (S and K), but have some influence on attitudes (A), through interactions with other managers, and by learning from the experiences of other course participants. Equally important was the training received on the job. People learn by doing. Here is how one of the managers we interviewed put it: "Hands-on experience and solving real work problems – that's how I developed my skills."

Our selection of the term *opportunities* was no accident. Implicit in it is the notion that one has to take full advantage of all training opportunities made available by the organization. I have seen a number of managers who looked upon training courses and workshops merely as time for rest and relaxation, a time to unwind and enjoy a short holiday!

Standards and feedback

I know you can do it.

This simple yet profound declaration from a manager to his or her employees had tremendous impact on some of the people we interviewed. High expectations, coupled with recognition of consequent success, were a key factor in their development. It is the well-known "self-fulfilling prophecy" at work: positive expectations and encouragement lead to positive results and higher motivation.

Moreover, managers who give more feedback and positive reinforcement, praising their employees more for good work and criticizing them less for making mistakes, tend to increase self-confidence and develop capabilities. One of the managers we interviewed told us that he uses a technique he learned from *The One Minute Manager*, by Kenneth Blanchard and Spencer Johnson (1982): "I try to catch my people doing something right!" Whatever techniques one uses to support and encourage subordinates, some sort of feedback on performance will surely be required to ensure that effective learning has taken place.

The knowledge base

The knowledge base refers to technical and organizational knowledge normally gained through diverse work experience. It also includes knowledge of the industry and the market in which the organization is engaged.

A study by Professor John Kotter (1988) concludes that one of the six basic requirements for effective leadership in senior management jobs is "broad knowledge of the industry and the company" (*The Leadership Factor*). Incidentally, Kotter's five other requirements were: relationships in the firm and industry; reputation and track record; abilities and skills; personal values; and motivation.

In our survey, a manager of a support department attributed his success to his understanding of the company's business:

> *Intimate knowledge of the company gave me the ability to empathize with line departments, the ability to be practical when dealing with engineers, and thus ask reasonable requests from them.*

Although the knowledge base is usually built and widened by practical and varied work experience, it is important to bear in mind that this experience should be evaluated by its richness and variety, not by the number of years or the number of promotions.

Formal career development

This ninth ingredient for success refers to formal HR systems where developmental activities are methodically planned for employees, in particular for high potential employees. Individual programs are designed to fill the gaps between the requirements of a job (professional and core competencies) and the existing capability of an individual employee. Career development programs are designed for individuals in their present positions; or for lateral moves; or, most likely, for promotions to new jobs.

These development programs usually include activities such as special projects or assignments, cross-functional moves, on-the-job training, leave relief or acting as a deputy, and formal training courses and seminars. A large number of the managers we interviewed linked their success to the experience and competencies they gained through such formal career development programs. The best remembered developmental activities were cross-posting to another company and cross-functional moves within the same company that lasted at least one year. Here is how one manager described the benefits of a crossfunctional move:

> *My move to Maintenance Department was of tremendous value. Having worked in the oil exploration side of the business and then going to Maintenance was like being a car designer and later becoming a garage mechanic . . . one gets to understand the whole process.*

The programs should have meaningful development activities that can be evaluated and measured on a periodic basis. Unfortunately, I have witnessed too many cases of young university graduates whose first development programs included such vague activities as "become familiar" or "get acquainted" with lists of tasks by visiting a number of departments for a few months each, only to end up becoming tourist trainees! These young people become either quickly de-motivated and frustrated, or worse yet, they may start believing that touring departments is what careers are all about!

The employee's performance must be periodically reviewed and the length of the career program adjusted accordingly. If monitored and managed well, career development and assessment of potential systems can reduce the all too common tendency of promoting people to their level of incompetence (Peter's Principle: In a hierarchy every employee tends to rise to his level of incompetence.)

In his book, *A Force for Change* (1990), John Kotter warns that "a long series of narrow and tactical jobs" or vertical career moves do not develop long-term and strategic skills. Instead, he recommends new job assignments, special development jobs, and lateral moves – which will broaden the knowledge base.

No discussion of career development would be complete without a word or two on the importance of self development, which was the fifth ingredient for success. One of the basic principles of management development is about providing opportunities for managers to develop themselves. Development takes place when the managers themselves are most motivated and committed to learn. The organization, line managers, and HR specialists create the learning opportunities and environment, but it is up to the individual to take full advantage of such opportunities. In short, *development is self-development*, to paraphrase Peter Drucker, the management expert.

A problem-solving culture

The last of the ten ingredients for success refers to an organizational environment or atmosphere where employees are actively involved in solving problems through open discussion and brainstorming; where organizational problems are used to teach people; where managers treat mistakes as opportunities for learning; and where finger-pointing, blame-fixing, and bureaucratic behavior are frowned upon.

It is a company culture that we nowadays call "a learning organization". It is a culture that ultimately earns the company the coveted reputation of being a preferred employer.

One of the managers in our study commenting on the subject of making mistakes:

I believe that an employee who is not making mistakes is probably not working hard! You are likely to find that the person who made no mistakes performed five or ten tasks, while his counterpart who made a few mistakes has carried out a hundred tasks.

The problem-solving culture reminds me of the anecdote of an international company, where a senior executive committed a costly mistake – his pet project failed, costing the company millions of dollars. Some people asked the Chief Executive Officer, "Aren't you going to fire him?" The CEO replied, "Are you crazy? I've just invested millions in training this man." Legend has it that this CEO was Thomas Watson, Sr., the founder of IBM.

"The fastest way to succeed," IBM's Thomas Watson, Sr., once said, "is to double your failure rate." In recent years, more and more executives have embraced this point of view, coming to understand what innovators have always known: that failure is a prerequisite to invention. A business can't develop a breakthrough product or process if it's not willing to encourage risk taking and learn from subsequent mistakes.
(R. Farson and R. Keyes, "The Failure-Tolerant Leader",
Harvard Business Review, August 2002)

A closing comment

The following few words from Kotter encapsulate some of the lessons learned from our discussion of the ingredients for success:

Instead of nurturing talent, encouraging people to lead and to learn from mistakes and successes, organizations all too often ignore leadership potential, offer no relevant training or role models, and punish those who make small errors while trying to lead. Individuals, too, get in their own way by failing to assess their developmental needs realistically and to proactively seek means of meeting those needs.

(Kotter, 1999)

What are the implications of our research findings? Clearly managerial success is more likely if all ten ingredients are present, but the data show that success is still possible with five or six of these ingredients. Naturally, it is preferable if the majority of the ingredients a person brings to the organization are from the first, more critical, five.

In brief, organizations can recruit and select people who have some or most of the first five ingredients, and then systematically make available to their employees the next five ingredients so that they can continue to learn, grow, and develop into competent managers and leaders. Senior management can create, with the help of HR professionals, an environment that supports the development of competencies. Moreover, they can link the organization's business plans and strategy with the types of competencies and experiences people need – thereby sharpening their new, and difficult to imitate, strategic advantage: their human capital.

Chapter Three

The tripod

On motivation and job performance

*There is more nonsense, superstition, and plain self-deception
about the subject of motivation than about any other topic.*
(Thomas Gilbert)

*Fifty per cent of motivation comes from within a person and fifty
per cent from his or her environment, especially from the
leadership encountered there.*

(John Adair)

I believe that motivation is one of the most over-used, misused,
and misunderstood concepts in business management. Many
books and various theories have attempted, with varying degrees
of success, to explain motivation. Why the difficulty? Here is a
simple and short answer: motivation is a multi-faceted, multi-
dimensional and complex concept. To fully understand it, one
has to see it from different perspectives, levels and viewpoints: it
is like looking at the proverbial elephant! One can only truly see

the elephant if one views it from different vantage points, from all angles and sides. This chapter will attempt to view motivation, this time using the metaphor of the tripod.

Let us begin by examining one of the many common misconceptions about motivation often found in popular business literature. This misconception suggests that managers can motivate *most* employees; and that these managers can accomplish this feat, by themselves, that is *on their own.*

The first part of the misconception assumes that managers, if only armed with the right techniques and skills, can motivate *most* employees. What about employees who are not self-motivated? Or employees who are not in the right jobs? Or employees who are for some reason disgruntled with their organization? It is highly questionable if motivational techniques alone could adequately deal with these and other similar problems.

Conventional wisdom says that it is far better for managers to find and recruit highly self-motivated employees, and keep them motivated, rather than waste time and resources trying to motivate non-self-motivated ones.

Two recent and excellent books make it clear that great leaders and managers are those who first *find and recruit* the best talent and then marshal it effectively. Steven Sample (2002) states that once great leaders identify and recruit their "lieutenants" they will "bend over backward" to help them get their job done. Buckingham and Coffman (1999) highlighted the importance of selecting the right talent. They state: "Selecting for talent is the manager's first and most important responsibility. If he fails to find people with the talents he needs, then everything else he does to help them grow will be wasted ..." Clearly, recruiting talented people who are already motivated is half the battle. Keeping them motivated is the other half. Of course, managers may not always have the luxury of recruiting or selecting their direct reports; more often than not most of one's employees are inherited!

The second part of the misconception is that managers *on their own* are responsible both for motivating their employees, and for keeping them motivated. Most of the popular "how-to-motivate" publications seem to ignore the enormous external constraints that are imposed on managers, and which in turn could cancel or greatly diminish their efforts when they try to motivate employees. These constraints may be imposed, for example, by the organization's policies and practices, excessive bureaucracy, restrictive governmental legislation, social and cultural factors, or changing economic conditions, any of which could severely de-motivate employees. It just seems unfair to place most of the burden on the manager's shoulder. I believe, therefore, that motivation is more of an organizational level issue, not to be relegated solely to the immediate manager's job.

The tripod and motivation

Some of the earliest and most extensively used theories on motivation explain behavior in terms of psychological needs, intrinsic and extrinsic motivation, or personal goals. Other, more recent, theories give more emphasis to the organizational culture (corporate environment and its systems), leadership, and so on. And therein lies the predicament of managers: Given the cultural variety and complexity of human beings, and the fact that they react differently to changing situations, which of the above schools of thought should guide them when managing people in the workplace?

At the core of an energized workforce is the quality of the one-on-one relationships that individual workers have with their managers, and the trust, respect, and consideration that their managers show toward them on a daily basis. Getting the best out of workers is above all a product of the "softer" side of management – how individuals are treated, inspired and challenged to do their best work – and the support, resources and guidance that is provided by managers to help make exceptional employee performance a reality.

(From *1001 Ways to Energize Employees*,
1997, by Bob Nelson)

Perhaps most important of all, you begin to realize that there is no right or wrong culture, no better or worse culture, except in relation to what the organization is trying to do and what the environment in which it is operating allows. General arguments of the sort you read in popular literature – about becoming more team-based, or creating a learning organization, or empowering employees – are all invalid unless they show how the basic assumptions on which these "new values" are based are adaptive to the environment in which the organizations have to function. In some markets and with some technologies, teamwork and employee empowerment are essential and the only way the organization can continue to succeed. In other market environments or with other technologies, tight discipline and highly structured relationships are the prerequisites to success. There is no best or right culture . . .

(From *The Corporate Culture Survival Guide*,
1999, by Edgar Schein)

Combining the two schools of thought will not do justice to either, and would almost certainly be a lengthy task, and perhaps too theoretical. Instead, it would be much easier to delineate and analyze the inter-relationships of motivation with other work-related factors. In other words, let us first try to put "motivation" in its fuller context.

Our interest in motivation stems from the premise that it affects performance on the job. It is, therefore, better to begin with performance itself, and then ask what influences it, that is, what are the *main people/human factors* that lead to higher performance?

Individual performance, I believe, is the product of three variables: ability (can do), motivation (willingness to do), and opportunity (chance to do). In brief, P = AMO, or

Performance = Ability × Motivation × Opportunity

Therefore, our concern is not motivation *per se* after all, but rather *how motivation contributes to improved performance*. I say "contributes" because either one of the two remaining variables could cancel out the performance of a highly motivated individual. Likewise, any competent employee with ample opportunities will not perform well if he or she is not motivated. All three variables are crucial.

Andy Grove, of Intel Corporation, almost got it right when he stated,

> *If an employee is not doing his job, there are only two possible explanations. Either he can't do it or he won't. To determine which, apply the following test: If the person's life depended on doing the work, could he do it? If the answer is yes, the problem is motivational. If the answer is no, the problem is lack of ability.*

However, if, according to John Adair, self-motivation accounts for fifty per cent of all motivation, then only that fifty per cent is represented in this AMO equation. What are the other factors that make up the remaining fifty per cent? Is motivation a stand-alone subject or are we trying to understand it better for other managerial purposes? Finally, what other cultural or organizational variables influence motivation most? I shall attempt to answer these questions using the *Tripod* metaphor. I must admit at the outset that the following analysis will be biased toward human resource management and the people side of management.

Imagine that an individual is a video camera placed on a tripod. Further, imagine that the three legs holding the camera are the immediate manager, the corporate culture, and the external environment. Those three legs make up the other fifty per cent of motivation.

Performance = Ability × Motivation × Opportunity
↓
↓
THE PERSON
Self-Motivation
(First 50%)

Immediate   Corporate   External
manager   culture   environment
                  (Second 50%)

Figure 3.1   Motivating managers

The three legs

There is no doubt that the immediate supervisor, manager or leader has the greatest impact on the motivation of employees or followers. Of course, they can motivate people by using the appropriate, and now well-known, motivational techniques. They may well be the epitome of a "super" supervisor, manager or leader. But what will happen to all these efforts if the corporate culture is really bad? For example, what if inter- or intra-departmental communication and teamwork are dismal? What if the human resources functions such as compensation, performance management, training, and career development are poorly run or non-existent? What if the organization is losing direction or is about to fold? And the list of unhealthy corporate practices can go on and on. I suggest that a poor corporate culture can indeed severely hamper or even wipe out the efforts of the immediate manager.

Similarly, if the immediate manager is doing an excellent job of motivating their team and if the corporate culture is healthy, uncontrollable events in the external environment can adversely affect any high motivation found among employees. Examples of external events include wars, severe economic recessions, unstable currency rates or price of crude oil, unreasonable governmental interference, hostile mergers or acquisitions, large layoffs, excessive head office control, revolutionary technological innovations and so on; not to mention some of the less desirable acts of Mother Nature. Any of these external factors will eventually impact morale and motivation negatively. Organizations are part and parcel of their environments; they don't operate in a vacuum.

To summarize, fifty per cent of motivation is self-motivation, and fifty per cent is influenced by the immediate manager, the corporate culture and the external environment. In order to stimulate discussion during our executive training programs, we ask participants which of the three is the most critical: immediate manager, corporate culture or external environment. Invariably, and after heated discussions, the majority would say that most of the weight ought to be given to the immediate manager, but they would quickly add the proviso that any major change in a particular organization (such as a change in top management), or a detrimental external event would surely lessen the weight initially attributed to the immediate manager. Therefore, motivating employees is not the sole responsibility of the immediate manager; he or she would need the full support of the organization and its leader or CEO.

Let us keep in mind that our goal is higher performance, and that motivation is only one part of the equation, although a very critical part. We will now briefly list what the immediate manager can and should do to motivate employees. We will also list some of the organizational support systems as well as some top management actions without which it would be difficult to harness and maximize the potential of motivated and competent people for *achieving high performance*.

The immediate manager

There are numerous publications, both theoretical and practical, which give advice to managers on how to motivate their associates or employees. This abundance of advice can perhaps be boiled down to a dozen or so items. I will list ten items, which I believe are most critical as well as culturally neutral:

1 Give recognition and rewards for good work
2 Set clear and challenging performance standards/targets/ outcomes
3 Provide feedback on a continuous basis

4 Train, coach and discuss career progress and opportunities
5 Treat each person well, and treat each person as an individual
6 Provide purpose for each job, and how it fits with the organization's vision
7 Ensure the right fit between individuals and jobs, then build on strengths
8 Consult and involve employees often; they know the intricacies of the job best
9 Hold people accountable, but allow them to learn from mistakes
10 Set a good example.

Sounds familiar? Of course! Thoughtful writers and excellent practicing managers have been describing these motivational techniques for many years; and I believe that these techniques are still applicable today notwithstanding the increasing rate of change and vast technological innovations. In other words, things have not really changed much from the early days of Maslow's hierarchy of needs and Herzberg's two-factor theory, to the more recent and excellent books on leadership. But perhaps there are nowadays more managers who are applying some of these old and new approaches to managing a more enlightened workforce, in a much more competitive world.

I recall when, over twenty-five years ago, as a junior member of Meirc's research team on motivation we called our findings **TPU: T** for treat us well: a good manager, according to the employees who were interviewed, would treat them in a considerate and humane manner. He or she would be interested and willing to provide good services and facilities, as well as care and guidance to their problems. **P** for pay us well: employees expected to be recognized and rewarded fairly, in line with their accomplishments and skills. **U** for use us well: employees expected to be trained in new skills; and to have their skills, knowledge and talent used in their present or future jobs.

It is gratifying to notice that TPU still covers several of the ten items mentioned earlier! But great managers will not only ask, "How can I motivate people?"; they will go on to ask, "How can I create the conditions within which these people will stay motivated?" Here is where the second leg, the corporate culture, comes in.

The corporate culture

Corporate culture refers to organizations' shared values, structure, systems and leadership style; it is the climate in which people work. Corporate culture's impact on motivation and performance can be very powerful, for better or worse. This was clearly shown in research carried out by many scholars including: Deal and Kennedy (2000); Collins and Porras (1994); Collins (2001); and Schein (1992).

In *Corporate Culture and Performance* (1992), Kotter and Heskett challenged the widely held belief that "strong" corporate cultures result in excellent business performance, showing that while many shared values and practices can promote good performance in some instances, those cultures can also be characterized by arrogance, inward focus, and bureaucracy – features that undermine an organization's ability to adapt to change. They also show that "healthy" cultures may not necessarily support excellent performance over long periods of time unless they adopt new strategies and practices in response to changing markets and new competition. In their opinion, this requires strong and effective leadership.

Similarly, the systems and practices used by the organization are derived from shared values and strong leadership. These include, but are not restricted to: performance measurement systems; human resource functions (recruitment, compensation, appraisal systems, training, career development and so on); the value placed on teamwork, open communication, innovation, quality, and customer service; the decision-making processes; and the organization's hierarchy and structure. Any or all of these can have severe adverse impact on motivation and performance if they are not aligned with the organization's purpose, strategy or technology.

I was recently asked to run a teambuilding workshop for senior managers of a large manufacturing company. The president of this company felt that members of his senior management team were not behaving like "team players": blaming each other and pointing fingers, stabbing each other in the back on occasions, reluctant to cooperate, and so on. After lengthy face-to-face discussions with each manager, I shared my conclusions and recommendations with the president. The main sources of the problem were structural in nature, and not simply due to lack of teamwork or personal reasons. The reward and recognition systems used by the company worked against teamwork because the performance of senior managers was measured and evaluated based on departmental achievements, which pitted sales against manufacturing, and manufacturing against maintenance – the classical conflicts between these departments were thus further exasperated!

The recommendations were to set, and measure, *team* performance targets derived from the strategic plans of the company; to assign multi-departmental task forces and project teams to tackle long-term problems or improvement schemes; and to cross-rotate a number of middle managers. Training, if still required, would follow later.

Coming back to self-motivated individuals, what if they happen to choose a career in an organization whose culture is not in line with their personality type or talent? Say, they do not thrive on teamwork when the organization demands it; or they cannot work well under tight discipline? And what if the management support systems, such as training and career development are poor or non-existent? Worse yet, what if the top executive has an autocratic management style or does not "walk the talk"? Surely, their motivation and their performance will suffer. Once again, the efforts of immediate managers at motivating some of their employees are in jeopardy.

Incidentally, it is usually the top leader, the CEO, who could possibly influence or shape corporate culture, and that usually takes an intensive effort over many years. Most first-line supervisors or middle managers are helpless when it comes to changing corporate culture. Again, it seems unwise to expect that motivating employees for higher performance is the sole responsibility of the immediate manager. That burden should be shared, though perhaps not equally, by all three legs of the tripod.

Finally, in certain countries in the world and in multinational companies, managers must take into account the fact that many of their employees come from many nations and different cultures. This requires a different, and perhaps a very special, managerial skill: managing and motivating a multi-cultural workforce. For example, in some companies in the Arab world the workforce includes expatriate employees from over 30 countries. The subject of managing a multi-cultural workforce will be covered in more detail in Chapter 4, The transit lounge.

The external environment

The external environment refers to the constraints and pressures from the many environments that organizations work in. The sources of pressure include political, economic, demographic, community and social factors, and the market/industry. The list of specific potential pressures is a long one. Here are the most common ones that I have observed over the years across different organizations and countries:

1 Headquarters' restrictions on subsidiaries or branches might be standard operating procedures, which are meant to fit all situations or business units, but are in fact restrictive in nature.
2 Joint venture partners, especially when partners are from different countries and cultures, resulting in conflict of interest in spite of good intentions.
3 Governmental bureaucracy and interference, as most strategic industries and services in developing countries (such as energy and airline companies) are still government owned or controlled, notwithstanding recent privatization efforts.
4 Restrictive governmental regulations, especially labor laws and practices which make employment termination of national employees in some countries extremely difficult. In addition, in certain countries, there are severe pressures stemming from nationalization or localization drives.
5 In hostile takeovers or mergers, especially when restructuring or downsizing, conflict and stress are likely.
6 Competitive threats, such as sudden new entrants to the market, or new technological breakthroughs.
7 Influence and demands by family and friends (personal ties and connections, or *wastah* as it is called in Arabic) in a wide range of business transactions, from hiring to awarding contracts, can be difficult problems.

What can be done to protect the organization from these external influences? Not too much. The Board of Directors, the CEO and the senior management team can shield the organization from some, but certainly not all, external pressures. Clearly, there are only a few situations where preventive actions or contingency plans could be put in place to lessen some of the harmful effects of external influences.

The external environment also refers to local or global unanticipated, or uncontrollable, events. Wars, recessions, globalization, and natural disasters come to mind. For example, when Iraqi "Scud" missiles were falling on Riyadh and on Jubail in Saudi Arabia, employees' morale and motivation were low. The expatriate workforce fled the industrial areas, leaving the Saudis in charge of running the petrochemical plants, while being handicapped by severe shortages of staff and concern for the lives and safety of their immediate family members.

Similarly, on a few occasions the price of crude oil fell to around $8 to $10 a barrel resulting in downsizing, budget cuts, freezing salaries, and slashing of perks and benefits which in turn caused widespread de-motivation. Once again, senior management is rather restricted in what it can do to protect the organization from such external events.

Some specific actions

Returning to the earlier analysis of performance, let us list some specific actions that I believe can be taken at both the managerial and organizational levels to enhance performance.

Recall:

Performance = Ability × Motivation × Opportunities

At managerial level (in addition to the ten items listed earlier):
• ensure that employees have the materials and equipment needed to do their job correctly

- identify training and developmental needs
- provide on-the-job training
- use delegation to train and motivate employees
- encourage and support self-development
- promote creativity, proactivity and initiative.

At organizational level:
- recruit and select the right talents and skills
- identify future training and developmental needs
- provide budgets, staff and facilities for training
- ensure that compensation is highly competitive, and that pay is mostly performance-based (including bonus or incentive pay)
- review your authority manuals and policies to ensure the widest possible participation and involvement of your employees in decision making and strategy formulation
- establish effective communication/information systems across the organization
- use modern performance management systems, with customized performance appraisal forms
- design career development systems to build on the strengths and potential of employees, with emphasis on lateral mobility and cross-training.

In short, it becomes critical nowadays to create a corporate strategy where your people become your strongest competitive advantage. This is the plea we have been hearing from business writers whose backgrounds include human resource management. The appeal has been stated by many, including Pfeffer (*The Human Equation: Building Profits by Putting People First,* 1998); Gratton (*Living Strategy: Putting People at the Heart of Corporate Purpose,* 2000); and Becker *et al.* (*The HR Scorecard: Linking People, Strategy and Performance,* 2001).

It seems that the success of the Balanced Scorecard approach for implementing strategy is partly due to the addition of three measures: *people, internal business processes* and *customers* rather than relying heavily, or solely, on financial performance measures. See *The Balanced Scorecard* (Kaplan and Norton 1996).

It has been said many times before that products, technology, and delivery practices can all be imitated or copied by competition, but not so with people! To get the best out of people, to motivate them, and to retain them requires corporate-wide systems and practices (culture) that support and reinforce the important day-to-day behavior of managers as they themselves work on keeping their people motivated.

Motivation is indeed like an elephant! We simply looked at it this time from a different vantage point, and within the larger context of improving performance.

Chapter Four

The transit lounge

Managing a multicultural staff

Every person is in certain respects:
  a. Like all other persons
  b. Like some other persons
  c. Like no other person.

(Kluckhohn and Murray, 1948)

There are truths on this side of the Pyrenees that are falsehoods on the other.

(Blaise Pascal, translated from French)

Picture in your mind's eye a busy transit lounge at a major international airport. You will see people of all nationalities waiting or rushing to depart for their final destinations. Some stay there a few moments, others for hours.

Now picture similar situations in a large number of companies operating in countries where there are manpower shortages. You will also see people of many nationalities working there for relatively short periods of time. At some of these companies in the Arabian Peninsula, for example, there are up to 40 nationalities on the payroll. It will not be surprising to find that foreign expatriates make up anywhere from 10 to 90 per cent of the workforce at some companies. Moreover, most expatriates work there for periods ranging from one to four years, very few until retirement.

The same is equally true of employees working for multinational organizations; they are moved frequently to and from foreign locations, rarely staying more than a few years in each. Global corporations such as Shell, BP, Nestlé, Exxon Mobil, GE, and Motorola, to name a few, rotate their staff frequently around the world either to their overseas locations or send them on loan (secondment) to local organizations. Moreover, locally hired employees are known to shift from one multinational organization to the other, especially among food manufacturing and consumer goods companies.

I know how it feels to be in that transit lounge. It happened when I was on secondment to a Gulf oil company for four years, and I observe it whenever I work with multinational and local companies, which I have been doing for more than twenty-five years. Being there, one is struck by both the diversity of nationalities and the mobility of the expatriates. A local executive of a large Gulf company once remarked: "We see them come, and we see them go ... the whole country, and our company in particular, is like a transit lounge." I never forgot that observation, and I often use it to discuss the implications of this phenomenon when conducting multicultural awareness courses.

Perhaps the most significant implication of the transit lounge is that managers working with a mobile and multinational workforce must use different managerial styles, and specific multicultural skills. Cultural awareness, bridging cultural differences and working with multicultural staff are the subjects of this chapter.

What is culture?

Social anthropologists popularized the concept of culture in the first half of the twentieth century. With the expansion of international trade, and later globalization, the second half witnessed an explosion of ideas and books on multinational business and cross-cultural interactions. Most writers on culture agree that human societies share universal problems such as people's relationships to time, nature, and other human beings. Over thousands of years different societies have developed their own unique solutions to these shared problems, and these solutions have been handed over from one generation to another.

Culture (organizational or national) is defined as a shared system of values, meanings, and practices. The various theories of culture can be illustrated, and perhaps simplified, by using three metaphors: software of the mind; an onion; and normal distribution. These metaphors were used by Geert Hofstede (1996, 2001); and by Fons Trompenaars and Charles Hampden-Turner (1997).

Culture as the software of the mind

It was Hofstede who called culture "the software of the mind" or mental programming. The programming starts at birth and is influenced by the family, school, and workplace and by the type of political system of the state. In brief, he discovered five dimensions of differences among national cultures. Hofstede writes: "A dimension is an aspect of culture that can be measured relative to other cultures." His five dimensions are:

1 Power distance
2 Collectivism versus individualism

3 Femininity versus masculinity
4 Uncertainty avoidance
5 Long-term versus short-term orientation

Each of the fifty countries covered by Hofstede was characterized by a score on each of the five dimensions; he went on to show how these dimensions were empirically sorted into thirteen clusters and three multi-country regions. Thus, persons from one country or cluster can compare themselves *vis-à-vis* another country or cluster on each of the five dimensions. For example, most Americans will score low on uncertainty avoidance ("let's be flexible", or "let's play it by ear"), while most Japanese will score very high, indicating a preference for clear rules and agreed methods ("better follow the standard operating procedures"). Americans will be low to medium on power distance (using first names or politely disagreeing with the boss), while Indians or Arabs will be higher on this dimension (high deference to boss).

The implications of Hofstede's studies for managerial practices are very significant: certain management systems (for example management by objectives (MBO)) or leadership theories (participative style perhaps) that work well in one culture are unlikely to be effective in others. The "software" and mental programs differ from one culture to another.

Culture as an onion

Both Hofstede and Trompenaars (1997) used the onion metaphor to depict the layers (or levels) of culture. The outer layers of the onion are what you observe at first encounters: artifacts, dress, food, language, monuments and other symbols of that culture; some call these the daily practices of a society and its people. As you peel the onion, the next layers represent the norms and values – the core – of the culture. Here we find a culture's definition of good versus bad, or right versus wrong, or normal versus abnormal, and so forth. Figure 4.1 depicts these ideas visually.

Trompenaars and Hampden-Turner (1997) warned of the danger of judging people when looking only at the outer layer of culture. They said: "Prejudices mostly start on this symbolic and observable (outer) level. We should never forget that each opinion we voice regarding explicit culture usually says more about where *we* come from than about the community we are judging" (emphasis added by the two authors).

This is how I illustrate the concept of the onion in my multi-cultural management classes: I ask a Western expatriate manager to imagine seeing a young national of an Arab Gulf country getting out of a Mercedes, wearing jeans, carrying an MP3 player, walking into a fast-food restaurant. You introduce yourselves to each other while waiting in the queue. It turns out that you work for the same large oil company. Let us suppose you share a table with this person, and you begin a social

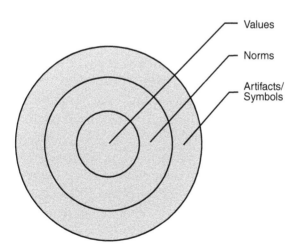

Figure 4.1 The onion image of culture

conversation (about sports or weather). This first layer of the onion may suggest a "Westernized" person. Perhaps it is true; but remember that this is only the outer layer of the onion. Later, you meet the same person at the company's social club and you discuss a more serious topic (say, friendship or work), cultural differences may start to surface especially when questions of right and wrong are invoked. If subsequently serious conversations (on family or religion) take place, deeper cultural differences may appear when it comes to issues of good and bad.

I have met many young non-Western managers over the years who have graduated from Western universities and who at first encounter seem to be quite "Westernized". Later discussions will reveal that only the outer layer was influenced by their Western educational experience. One really needs to peel the onion, to discover the core values, in order to gain greater awareness and understanding of cultural differences.

Incidentally, it is widely believed that core values are stable and consequently enduring, thus more difficult to influence or change; a point worth keeping in mind when interacting with people of different cultures.

Culture as a normal distribution

Trompenaars and Hampden-Turner described the concept of culture as a normal distribution in these words:

> *People within a culture do not all have identical sets of norms and values. Within each culture there is a wide spread of these. This spread does have a pattern around an average. So, in a sense, the variation around the norm can be seen as a normal distribution. Distinguishing one culture from another depends on the limits we want to make on each side of the distribution.*
>
> (Trompenaars and Hampden-Turner, 1997)

The often-cited quotation from Kluckhohn and Murray (1948) that appears at the beginning of this chapter warrants a brief comment. Of course, this quotation is a truism: no one would deny that every person is in certain respects like *all* other persons (similarities among humankind); every person is in certain respects like *some* other persons (same culture or profession); and every person is in certain respects like *no* other person (unique personality).

It also relates to the normal distribution idea, and it warns us of the perils and limits of cultural stereotyping. For example, not all Arabs attach a low value to time, and not all Japanese value time highly. However, the Japanese, in general, place a higher value on time than the Arab, on average. See Figure 4.2.

National contrasted with organizational culture

As Hofstede (1996) once wrote: "Effective multinationals have created practices that bridge the national value differences .... Common practices, not common values are what solve practical problems." He went on to say: "An organization is a social

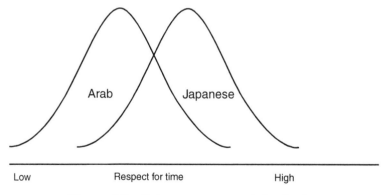

Figure 4.2 Culture as a normal distribution

system of different nature than a nation; if only because the organization's members usually have a certain influence in their decision to join it, are only involved in it during working hours, and may one day leave it again."

Employees of multinational companies transfer frequently from one region (or branch) to the other. For example, a Swiss citizen working for Nestlé may be transferred to new locations every three or four years. Incidentally, these employees are challenged to re-learn the new markets and customers, and to adjust to the management styles practiced at their new destinations.

A regional director of a multinational company, who was based in Dubai, described working for such companies in these words: "Individual performance is the common denominator in all these companies. However, some multinationals valued personality style and character traits in addition to performance; while in others it was strictly performance."

The locally hired employees of multinational companies also experience the transit lounge phenomenon. They are commonly, and I think crudely, known as third country nationals (TCNs). In the Gulf region, I have known many Indians, Pakistanis, Filipinos, and nationals of various Arab countries who have changed jobs from one multinational company to another. The multinational companies which I refer to include Lucent, Procter and Gamble, Pepsi Cola, Mars (American); Nestlé (Swiss); Unilever (British and Dutch); BP (British); Schlumberger (French) and Sony (Japanese), to name a few.

One of our favorite discussions with these locally hired employees is to ask them to compare the corporate cultures of their past and present multinational employers. The observations these middle managers made were along these lines:

- It took a few months, but I adjusted to the faster pace here.
- There is job security here; with my previous employer, we never had it.
- In this company they look closely at the bottom line, and they want quick results.
- Here you are given more room for innovations and new ideas.
- We all work longer hours, but the pay and perks are great!
- These guys believe in training – I've been on so many courses since I joined.
- It is much more casual in this company, first name basis!
- Definitely less centralized than the case with my previous employer.

From society to society, country to country, nation to nation, the approach to management differs. It differs in the way authority is used, in interpersonal relationships on the job, in communications style, in assertiveness, in speed of action, in bureaucratization, and much more. Even at the center of what seems to be the common core, the formal structures of organizations can vary in terms of the number of layers and number of departmental specialisms.

(David J Hickson, *Exploring Management across the World*, 1997)

My personal observations over many years of working with multinational companies have led me to believe that it is difficult to generalize about the extent to which national cultures influence (or are influenced by) the cultures of multinational organizations. Instead, it is perhaps simpler to think of each organization's overseas operation as a different type of transit lounge where you find employees of many nationalities adapting to the practices/culture of that specific transit lounge. Always learning or re-learning the ropes! At the same time, corporate practices of multinationals adapt to the host country's local characteristics, legislation, workforce, and culture. Effective multicultural managers, it seems, are those who are culturally sensitive (with plenty of empathy), global in outlook, and have excellent cross-cultural communication skills.

Charles Handy described organizational culture in these words:

> *In organizations, there are deep-set beliefs about the way work should be organized, the way authority should be exercised, people rewarded, people controlled. What are the degrees of formalization required? How much planning and how far ahead? What combination of obedience and initiative is looked for in subordinates? Are there rules and procedures or only results? These are all parts of the culture of an organization.*
>
> (Handy, 1993)

Working with expatriates

Now we flip the coin and discuss the expatriates working in national, local organizations, *not* employees of multinational corporations. These expatriates are usually on employment contracts with organizations in countries that suffer from manpower shortages. For example, in the six countries of the Arabian Gulf Cooperation Council, such expatriates make up around 70 per cent of the total workforce. Although most of these expatriates work for the private sector in construction, services and sales jobs, many are working for the major employers (oil and gas industries or government) in administrative and technical positions at the lower, supervisory, and managerial levels. Depending on the country, the number of expatriates working for the various Gulf oil and gas companies ranges from 10 to 90 per cent of the workforce.

How are these expatriates perceived by their hosts? In our research of 1989 and 2002, we asked Gulf national managers who worked for, worked with, or supervised expatriates, "What are the characteristics of expatriates which you most admire and dislike." For the purpose of our research, we classified expatriates in three categories: *Western* expatriates, mostly from Europe; *Arab* expatriates; and *Asian* expatriates, mostly from the Indian subcontinent and Philippines. It is important to note, at the outset, that many Gulf managers felt their answers did not necessarily apply to *all* Western, Arab, or Asian expatriates. Many qualified their statements by saying: "Of the ones I admire, these are the characteristics which I admire most." Examples of the characteristics, which they disliked, were similarly qualified.

As we shall see shortly, the responses to this question could help both Gulf managers and expatriates. These responses, I believe, tell us as much about the host managers as they do about the expatriates. For the expatriates, receiving feedback about their image could help reduce the cultural barrier, and it may speed the adaptation and adjustment process. Tables 4.1a and 4.1b are summaries of the findings, listed in the order of frequency of mention.

Most of the responses are self-explanatory; however some warrant a few brief remarks. "Hard work" was an admired characteristic in all three groups. Other common admired characteristics were "expertise", "discipline and respect for time", and "technical competence". One can perhaps speculate that the characteristics most admired by the Gulf managers are those that managers wish to see more of in their own national colleagues and subordinates. This was indeed the explanation that many of the Gulf managers who attended our courses gave when presented with these responses.

Table 4.1a Expatriates as perceived by Gulf managers, *most admired* characteristics

Western expatriates	Arab expatriates	Asian expatriates
1 Know-how, expertise and experience	Same culture, language and habits	Hard work and willingness to do any type of work
2 Hard work, dedication to work and ability to concentrate	Friendly, sociable and humanitarian	Technically competent, especially at technical jobs
3 Professionalism and managerial skills	Loyalty and trustworthiness	Well disciplined
4 Discipline and respect for time	Hard work	Good desk people (especially for routine and clerical work)
5 Organization, precision and attention to detail	Decisiveness	Perseverance

Table 4.1b Expatriates as perceived by Gulf managers, *most disliked* characteristics

Western expatriates	Arab expatriates	Asian expatriates
1 Arrogance, sense of superiority, "their way is the only and best way"	Too emotional and talkative	Block knowledge and information, and hinder development of nationals
2 Lack of respect for Arab/Muslim way of life	Cliquish – tend to form "in-groups" at work	"Yes" men, overly obeisant, do not challenge instructions, or stand up for their rights
3 Materialistic: here only for the money	Hinder development of nationals	Not very creative, prefer routine work
4 Cliquish, "in-group", no desire to mix with other nationalities (at or outside work)	Low value for time: not too punctual	Cliquish "mafia" formation
5 Opposition to (and lack of interest in) the training and development of nationals	Weak on analysis and attention to details	Weak on leadership and decision making

Two problematic characteristics

There were two most disliked characteristics common to the three groups: cliquism and a reluctance to train and develop nationals. Both characteristics are natural and anticipated human behavior, given the nature of expatriation. Neither one is likely to be completely eliminated: they can, however, be managed and their detrimental effects minimized. Since both characteristics are, to some extent, inter-related they will be addressed together.

Expatriate cliques are social and organizational informal groups whose main purposes include satisfying the social and belonging needs, especially acute among people who are away from their home countries, and preserving national and personal identity. Cliques serve not only to satisfy the security and social needs, but also to reduce the initial culture shock and the subsequent feeling of being a resident alien. It would indeed be unusual for an expatriate, except for the rare cosmopolitans, not to actively belong to his national clique.

From the management point of view, of more importance is the function commonly acquired by expatriate cliques within the organization, namely, to protect jobs for their own nationals. Although expatriates will initially join a group to meet their socio-psychological needs, they may soon become actively involved in taking steps to avoid losing their jobs to nationals of the host country, or promoting the employment of their fellow expatriates.

The key to managing this phenomenon is to reduce uncertainty and job insecurity through the use of (a) employment contracts, specifying the length of stay in the host country, during which time an expatriate is contractually obligated to train nationals; and/or (b) develop a reward system based on how well and how soon an expatriate trains his replacement or successor. Several companies in the Gulf region have successfully used both methods. Cliques will always exist, and to some extent they are beneficial if used well, and their powerful networks are utilized for the benefit of the organization.

Further reactions to perceived characteristics

Finally, most of the other disliked characteristics can be eliminated or alleviated by careful recruitment and screening and well designed short courses. There are some courses designed for expatriates and their spouses before they arrive in their new host country, and others designed for expatriates and spouses six to nine months after they arrive.

Other courses bring together expatriates with their national host, during which erroneous perceptions and stereotyping by *both* sides may be discussed and corrected. At some companies, courses were held for Arab nationals with the objective of gaining deeper understanding of Western culture. These courses covered topics such as Western work ethics and mannerism, managerial styles, and even body language! In short, enhancing cultural awareness and improving the cross-cultural skills of *both* expatriates and nationals can be beneficial to all parties.

A checklist for managing and motivating expatriate staff

Being a manager in a transit lounge requires cultural sensitivity and specific managerial skills. This is mainly due to the high mobility and turnover of the staff, and their multicultural diversity.

The following checklist was developed from both my personal experience of being a manager of expatriates, and from the research conducted at Meirc in the Gulf region. Most of the points are, of course, an integral part of successfully managing any workforce; some are specific to managing employees from other cultures.

- Understand, appreciate and respect the expatriate's culture, mentality and feelings. For example, be aware of the special circumstances of the expatriate, who is not only concerned about job performance but has to learn the "new ropes" both at the company and in the new country (known as acculturation). In the meantime, the expatriate may also be trying to cope with pressures from spouse and children as they themselves try to adapt to the host country. A spouse's failure to adapt to the new culture has been found to be a major contributor to failed overseas assignments. Finally, there is the problem and anxiety of what will happen when an expatriate returns home – the re-entry problem. Expatriates who have been overseas for a long time seem to be out of favor at headquarters when they return; they have to re-learn the ropes and re-establish networks, an especially acute problem for Japanese managers.
- Ensure that nationals and expatriates are given equal interpersonal treatment. There is a tendency to start favoring one nationality over another, and this becomes quickly known and frowned upon. In fact, about 25 per cent of the managers we interviewed during our research warned about this specific danger. The advice here is to avoid favoritism between nationals and expatriates in terms of interpersonal relations and attitude. To many readers this advice is common sense, but it takes on added weight when managing and motivating a multinational staff.
- Vary the management style according to the nationality of the employee and the situation. Ken Blanchard's Situational

Leadership II provides four such styles: directing, coaching, supporting and delegating. (See www.kenblanchard.com). According to Blanchard's model, the variables that influence the recommended styles are the types of decision or situation, as well as the competence and development level of the employee. Culture, I believe, is another equally important factor to consider mainly because the *expectations* and *needs* of the employees themselves vary from culture to culture.

- Cross-cultural communication requires the ability to listen, to be open-minded, and to give and receive feedback. Although again this is common sense, it is particularly difficult when one communicates with people of different perceptions and "mental programs", not to mention different languages.

- Set clear expectations and responsibilities early on. Most expatriates going through a transit lounge expect to receive clear definitions of their jobs, performance targets, responsibilities and authorities. However, if given adequate and frequent feedback their anxiety will be alleviated on issues that they care about and are motivated by, such as pay, job security, career advancement, mobility, and marketability.

When all is said and done, it seems that for a long time to come cultural factors will exert a strong influence on managerial practices in transit lounge environments. This influence will be less on technical and production decisions, less on job design, and financial methods; but much more on motivation of employees, patterns of thought and communication, and styles of leadership. Globalization and the proliferation of multinational business will simply increase the diversity and mobility of people working in transit lounges around the world.

Chapter Five

The mosaic

Management in the Arabian Gulf countries

Time present and time past
Are both perhaps present in time future
And time future contained in time past.

(T S Eliot)

Men's natures are alike; it is their habits that carry them far apart.
(Confucius)

My first book, *The Arab Executive* (1980), was originally written as a Ph.D. thesis at the London Business School, University of London. I would like to share with you the main reason for choosing this particular subject.

After obtaining a Master's of Business Administration (MBA) from the University of California, Berkeley, I worked for almost six years as a manager with an American manufacturing firm in both California and Texas. My career with this firm was challenging, successful, and rewarding. Yet, when I started a new career in the Arab world, it became exceedingly clear that the management styles that I used with my American associates were not as effective with associates of other nationalities. Something was different; and I became inquisitive. Was it me, or was it the Western management styles that I was using? Why were most of the Western expatriates working in the Arab world seemingly successful? What were they doing differently? Did they have to adjust/adapt their styles to their foreign environment, and if so, how? Too many questions, yet very few answers were readily available at that time.

It was with this mindset that I started the Ph.D. program in London. In those days, the conventional wisdom was (and had been since the 1950s) that management systems and styles are universal. Researchers and gurus had been engaged in a debate over the extent to which Western (usually American) management styles and practices were exportable to other cultures. My own hypothesis was that management styles and practices might indeed differ from culture to culture, especially on those aspects that deal with people and interpersonal relations.

The findings of *The Arab Executive* strongly suggested, "... that certain managerial styles and skills required in the Arab world may differ from those advocated or practiced in Western cultures .... Indeed some of the Western managerial practices may not only be inapplicable but may be harmful if applied without adaptation to Arab environments." Has the passage of time since then brought any significant changes in management practices and styles? Partly to answer this question, Meirc Training & Consulting carried out a second major research entitled *The Making of Gulf Managers* (1989). Other than some minor changes, to be discussed later, the findings of the Meirc study confirmed the earlier study of Arab executives. Namely, that certain management practices and styles tend to be culturally specific. Again, in 2002, we re-visited and updated the main parts of the earlier studies. In this chapter, we shall summarize the findings of the three studies and point out the patterns and trends in management practices in the Arab world, with particular emphasis on the six Arabian countries who are members of the Gulf Cooperation Council (GCC). Let us begin by looking at the social landscape – a colorful mosaic depicting the wider environments and various cultures found in that part of the world. (See note at the end of this chapter for the origin of the mosaic metaphor as it relates to the Middle East).

The manager and his environment

When conducting research, I have always preferred to start at the macro level of culture and environment, and later zoom in and focus on management practices and styles at the organizational and individual levels. A great deal is learned by examining first the larger context, the wider environments in which organizations and their executives work. One way of conceptualizing the relationship between business executives and their various environments is shown in Figure 5.1. Of course, one must bear in mind that this conceptual separation is only meant to simplify social reality and aid in its analysis. Nevertheless, I have found it a useful framework to study management in any culture. It starts with an examination of the elements that make up the socio-cultural environment: the history, religion, social structure, values, norms, traditions, and customs; in short, culture. Depending on the regional culture under study, one can add as many environments as necessary; for my purposes, I included three other environments: political/governmental, economic, business and social community.

As in all cultures, each of the various environments imposes certain pressures on managers. What differ from culture to

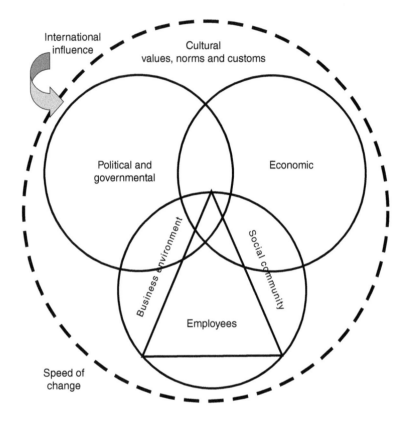

Figure 5.1   Managers and their various environments

culture, however, are the *types* and *strengths* of pressures, which in turn influence the thinking and behavior of managers. At this point, several examples are sufficient to demonstrate the variety of pressures. There are no labor unions in four out of the six GCC countries (Kuwait and Bahrain allow labor unions), whereas labor relations are a very serious matter for managers to consider in, for instance, the UK or Germany. In most of the Arabian Gulf, it is incredibly difficult to fire a national employee, while in the USA downsizing and firing employees during economic slowdowns are frequent events. In the Gulf countries, women make up only 5 to 6 per cent of the workforce, whereas in some Western countries this figure is around 50 per cent. In the Gulf, expatriate employees make up around 70 per cent of the workforce, a figure that is unheard of in any other country in the world. Corporate and individual income taxation hardly exists in the Gulf, while tax rates can reach 50 or 60 per cent in some Western countries. Finally, although the GCC countries are trying their best to reduce their reliance on oil and gas, their economies are still highly dependent on this one source of income.

As expected, the various environments are themselves undergoing change. However, it is the *speed* of change that has been remarkable in the Arabian Gulf ever since the discovery of oil in the 1930s and 1940s. This anecdote will perhaps illustrate the point. I was once flying from Dhahran in the Eastern province of Saudi Arabia to Jeddah, which is located on the Red Sea. Shortly after take off, the Saudi pilot made the usual public announcement about altitude, weather and expected time of arrival, and then he said something to this effect, "When I was a young boy, my family and I traveled the same distance on camels and it certainly took us much longer than two hours!" Here is a person flying a Boeing 747 who used camels for transportation 40 years earlier!

The population of the United Arab Emirates has increased 35-fold since 1950, and the area of the city of Riyadh has grown 100-fold. In Oman, electricity output has risen 670 times over the past 30 years, the number of telephones 420 times and the number of doctors 260 times. In Qatar, average incomes have grown 50-fold since 1960, and average wealth 200-fold.

(*The Economist*, 23 March 2002)

Meanwhile, the rush towards economic development and modernization continues in the Arabian Gulf, balanced by strong feelings that this must be accomplished without sacrificing traditions. In a recent survey of the Gulf, *The Economist* concluded its coverage on the subject of religion and modernity with this statement:

> *Struck by a tidal wave of change, Gulf Arabs are looking for certainties to cling to. At the same time the region's societies are proud of their resilience. "We are part of the world", says an advisor to the Saudi Ministry of Planning. "We cannot live alone. If we resist pressure, it is not because we are Islamic. We want to preserve our values like everyone else".*
>
> (*The Economist*, 23 March 2002)

Will Gulf societies and their institutions be able to maintain this mixture, or rather delicate coexistence, of the traditional and modern ways of life? Clearly, there is no easy answer to this question. Perhaps time will tell whether such a mixture is feasible or durable.

Finally, the environments where Gulf managers live and work have been under great international influence for some time. Other than the fact that the world has become far more open and accessible through the media, Internet, and extensive foreign travel, there are a large number of international companies and expatriates working and living in the Gulf area. Gulf managers, many of whom studied or were trained overseas, have become reasonably familiar with both Western and Eastern civilizations.

Problems and social pressures

One of the more serious problems facing the Gulf region is, and has been for years, the shortage of a skilled workforce (see Table 5.1). Even more important, this problem is nowadays further compounded by the fact that at the same time there is a growing unemployment among Gulf nationals. The outlook for this imbalance looks bleak, especially for those hundreds of thousands of high school and university students who are now in the pipeline and will be seeking jobs upon graduation. There are three main reasons for this potentially dangerous situation – a "time bomb", according to a recent statement by a Saudi government minister. First, the cost to employers of hiring expatriate workers is much less – although it is a heavy burden on the national economies since expatriates send home billions of dollars in remittances every year. Second, many local graduates lack the technical skills required by industry and business, as a large number of nationals have been studying arts

Table 5.1   Gulf Cooperation Council population and workforce

Country	Total 2002* population (in thousands)	Non-citizens as percentage of total population	Expatriates as percentage of workforce**
Bahrain	650	40	64
Kuwait	2,300	64	81
Oman	2,400	26	55
Qatar	720	80	90
Saudi Arabia	23,000	27	55
UAE	3,300	82	90

Notes: * Forecast; ** Estimate

Sixty per cent of the Gulf's national population is under the age of 25, and around 40 per cent is under 15. Most expatriates come from India, Sri Lanka, Pakistan, Egypt, and the Philippines.

Source: *The Economist*, 23 March 2002

and humanities rather than science and business. Third, although the Gulf has an abundance of its own high achievers and hard workers, it seems that many recent graduates are seen by employers as lacking discipline, motivation or willingness to do manual jobs.

Governments in the Gulf are now becoming far more serious about their nationalization or localization campaigns. However, I believe that the problem will be best tackled if: (a) the quality of education improves; (b) the educational systems start catering to the needs of industry; and (c) the difficulty of firing nationals is dramatically reduced. Finally, although the number of women in the workforce is slowly increasing, the problem will be somewhat alleviated as more women enter the job market.

Gulf women have made significant strides in the work arena in the past few decades. Although their total numbers remain small, Gulf women are working not only in the traditional sectors of education and health, but have also made good progress in banking and financial services, oil and gas industries, e-commerce and information technology, to name a few. For example, in May 2002, when an Omani woman was appointed as chairperson of a large national bank, the statement issued by the bank said, the new chairperson "has the distinction of being the first woman in Oman to head a board of directors in a corporate business". Of course, there are many other examples of Gulf women occupying high-level posts, especially in Bahrain, Kuwait and the UAE.

Nationalization of jobs requires – and certainly deserves – carefully designed systems of succession planning and career development. Nevertheless, in our experience with designing and implementing such systems, we have found that the biggest weakness and the poorest results are usually due to the lack of top management involvement, commitment or control. Consequently, this often leads to speeding up of nationalization programs, which, in turn, leads to inadequate outcomes. It is like driving a vehicle at a much higher speed than designed, and without proper maintenance, for long periods. Other than the detrimental dilution of experience in the organization or in the department, national employees tend to be promoted to higher positions before reaching the required levels of competence.

Indeed, this is one of the more serious problems mentioned by Gulf managers. Here are some of the other problems facing them and other managers in their organizations:

- subordinates lacking experience (due to fast pace of nationalization or poor qualifications)
- excessive rules, regulations and procedures (bureaucracy)
- lack of authority to make decisions (centralization)
- interference and restrictions from outside the organization (external influence from friends, family and government)
- people have low value and respect for time
- excessive use of favoritism and connections (*wastah*).

The twin problems of bureaucracy and centralization became more apparent at the end of the boom years in the mid-1980s. One possible explanation for their emergence at the start of the economic slowdown, when crude oil prices plummeted to around $8 per barrel, is that governments and companies embarked on serious campaigns to rationalize expenditure. This required curtailing or withdrawing the spending authorities of managers, accompanied by increasing amounts of "paperwork" and "rules and procedures" to justify expenditure, to obtain additional approvals, or to document the decision process for the record in the event of future questions. Nowadays, there is a gradual move towards e-government, particularly in Dubai, and wider use of electronic data systems in the private sector – all of which is easing the "paperwork" problem to some extent.

Pressures and interference from both governments and citizens are on the increase especially in the sensitive areas of employment of nationals and replacement of expatriates. The external influence problem is being exacerbated by the rising unemployment among nationals, and by the recent government campaigns to increase the percentage of nationals in the workforce.

The influence of family and friendship is still pervasive and significant in business management. Here are typical quotations on this subject from some managers we interviewed:

We tend to be closer because of our social environment . . . closely-knit families . . . everyone knows everyone else.

What 'people might say' influences decisions and behavior . . . we live in a small and close society.

Wastah (that is use of connections*) is killing us!*

It is easier to say no to a brother, but more difficult to say the same to a friend.

Friendship means a lot; it is an influential factor at work and in the majlis (the traditional guest lounge).

Finally, the problem of "low value and respect for time" seems to be diminishing in importance, whereas it was considered as a major problem years ago in the earlier study. This diminishing importance may perhaps be an indication that employees, and people in general, are becoming more professional in their outlook and more disciplined in the management of their time.

A drift towards power sharing?

Decision making is considered by many a prime factor in management. The often-made statement that managerial decision making is *the* organizational activity that matters has motivated researchers from a variety of disciplines to its study. Of course, there are many methods and styles in which decisions are made. Rarely is there one correct method or style that can be universally applied to all decisions in all situations. In fact, research suggests that decision-making styles are dependent on the interaction between cultural, situational and personal variables – often termed the situational approach.

Managers vary their styles in accordance with the problem or decision at hand, as common sense suggests. Thus, the style selected for a certain decision depends on several factors, the most important are: the manager's age; educational, social and cultural background; work level and experience; and his or her personality type. It also depends on the manager's subordinates: their socio-cultural background; their level of experience and expertise; their maturity; and whether there is a need to get their commitment to the decision. Additionally, the style used depends on the corporate culture, which refers to organizations' shared values, structure, systems and leadership style; it is the climate in which people work. Finally, the style used depends on the nature of the decision under consideration: its confidentiality; level of importance, urgency, scope and complexity; and whether a multi-disciplinary approach is considered necessary to make the decision – such as advice or input from finance, marketing, production, and so on. Nevertheless, it would seem reasonable to expect that managers have a natural and preferred style, which is more or less adaptable to various decisions or problems.

For the 2002 research, we used the same conceptual framework for classifying decision-making styles as that used in the earlier two studies (Muna, 1980 and Meirc, 1989), namely, a power-sharing continuum. This four-point scale indicates the extent to which managers share their power of decision making with their subordinates. The four styles on the continuum are:

I: Own decision   II: Consultation   III: Joint decision   IV: Delegation

A fuller description of the styles is included in the Interview Schedule and the Questionnaire (see Appendix).

Managers were asked to indicate which of the four styles:

(a) they felt is the most effective,
(b) they preferred to work under, and
(c) they felt their own manager's style most closely corresponded.

Figure 5.2 summarizes the data collected by the 2002 study; it shows the percentages of responses for the 181 Arab managers who participated in the research.

How do these results compare with the findings of the 1989 study? As can be seen from Figures 5.3 and 5.4, there are significant shifts in, first, what managers felt to be the *most effective* styles, and second, for the styles they *prefer to work under*. The shifts are towards more joint decision and delegation styles, and less consultation.

Undoubtedly, the managers who participated in the 2002 study were clamoring for power sharing, much more than their counterparts in the 1989 study. However, is power sharing actually taking place? Are their own managers involving them more in the decision-making process? Figure 5.5 shows a trend over the past two decades of less consultation and more joint decision. Consultation dropped from 55 to 44 per cent, and joint

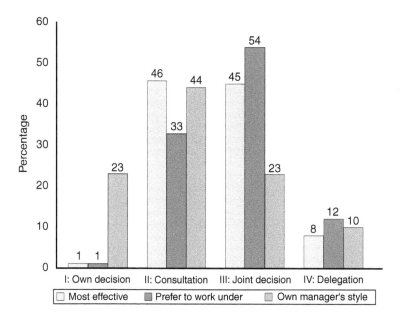

Figure 5.2 Responses for the decision-making styles (2002 study)

decision increased from 13 to 23 per cent. We can conclude that there is indeed a slow drift towards power sharing.

The slow drift towards more power sharing in decisions may be the result of a combination of factors influencing both managers and subordinates, such as:

• an increase in management education and training, and exposure to other cultures
• an increase in industrial experience and organizational maturity
• recent technological advances and the information revolution
• socio-cultural changes that encourage more involvement and participation.

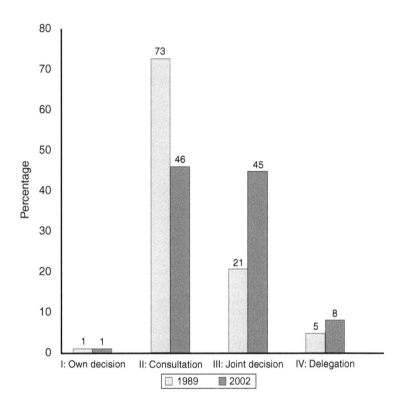

Figure 5.3   Comparison of the *most effective* decision-making styles (1989 and 2002)

Nevertheless, the results of these three studies confirm that Gulf managers are still somewhat frugal when it comes to sharing their decision-making power. Whether managers use Style I (own decision) or Style II (consultation), they essentially retain the decision-making power, since consultation is followed by a decision that may or may not have been influenced by the opinion of those who were consulted. Thus, for our present purposes, we can label the combination of Styles I and II as "autocratic-consultative". This means that the

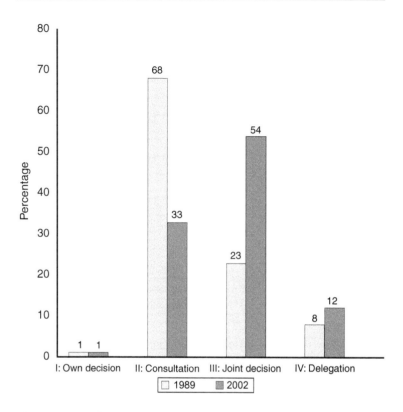

Figure 5.4 Comparison of the *prefer to work under* decision-making styles (1989 and 2002)

"autocratic-consultative" Styles I and II have dropped from 77 per cent in 1980 to 73 per cent in 1989 and to 67 per cent in 2002 (See Figure 5.5).

Our findings are very much in line with other research carried out in Gulf countries. Studies by Ali and Swiercz (1986), Ali and Schaupp (1992), Ali *et al.* (1997), and Yousef (1998) found strong preference for the "autocratic-consultative" decision-making styles. In all of these studies, as in ours, the consultative style alone ranged from 43 to 67 per cent.

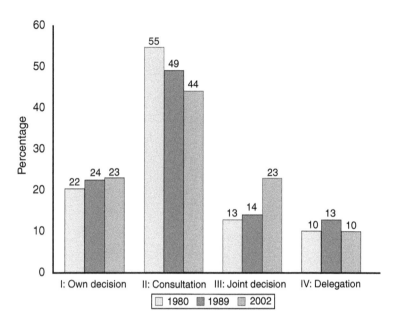

Figure 5.5   Comparison of the *own manager's* decision-making styles (1980, 1989 and 2002)

Why is the consultative decision-making style favored by Gulf managers? Consultation has historical, social and religious roots in the Arabian Gulf. Tribal leaders and heads of clans and families still consult important family members or influential friends on critical issues before making a decision. The final decision, incidentally, is typically made by the leader who may or may not adhere to the advice of his closest associates. Additionally, Islam actively encourages the use of consultation (*Shura*) through both the Holy Quran and the Hadith. In fact, one of the 114 chapters of the Holy Quran is entitled *Consultation*.

Management styles and practices in the Gulf

One of the distinctive features of management in the Gulf is the strong preference for a personal or person-oriented approach. Of course, there are in the Gulf, as in the rest of the Arab world, institutions and organizations that have formal rules and procedures and are supposed to run on impersonal basis, but these formal organizations are facades behind which one finds a lot of informality and personalized way of doing business. In fact, many Gulf managers have an aversion to impersonal relationships. Often, doing business requires extensive use of personal (family, friendship or tribal) ties and connections – things are simply done faster with the help of personal ties. Many managers practice, or claim to practice, the open-door policy, whereby employees in the organization can meet top managers or department heads. Employees seem to be motivated in direct proportion to the amount of personal attention they receive. This personal approach is sometimes used by managers not only in relations with employees but also with people outside the organization.

In keeping with socio-cultural norms of the area, the employer–employee relationship tends to be somewhat paternalistic – in a tribal or family manner. The employer (manager) feels that he is the head of the family or tribe: he is sometimes expected to provide care, guidance, advice and control in the same way that one would look for such treatment from an elder brother, father or uncle. One of the managers once told us "I give my employees the feeling of belonging to one family .... Many of the employees see me as a father." Another talked about being the "head of the family" or "tribe". Others talked about visiting their employees at home during particularly happy or sad occasions, or in hospitals if they fall ill.

Finally, since most Gulf managers work with, and manage, multicultural workforces, it would be worthwhile to look briefly at the relationship between Gulf managers and expatriates. This topic was discussed at length in Chapter 4, The transit lounge. The six Gulf countries, as noted earlier, rely to a large extent on expatriate workers and professionals. This is likely to continue for many years, despite the future influx of national graduates from schools and universities. Gulf managers, therefore, must be well trained to work with expatriates from a variety of countries.

I believe that Gulf managers should be trained on cross-cultural relations. Do Gulf managers, for example, know why Western or Eastern expatriates behave in certain ways that are in some cases seen as inhumane, impersonal, or even rude? Do they recognize all the differences that exist in values and beliefs especially when it comes to work ethics, work habits, or respect for time? Most of the well-seasoned Gulf managers have picked up that sort of knowledge the hard way, through years of exposure and on-the-job experience. What about the young graduates, some of whom will become future managers of expatriates?

Consider this fictional case of Martin, a young European expatriate with a successful record of accomplishment who was recently assigned to a supervisory job in the Gulf. His national subordinates misinterpreted his well-meaning, but demanding and impersonal style. He was very conscientious about his job, and believed in the principle that "time is money". When frustrated with the new work environment, he would become pushy, and at times lose his patience. In short, Martin was a performance-oriented supervisor, who was looking forward to a rewarding experience abroad. However, this is how he was perceived by his subordinates, most of whom were technicians in his Maintenance department:

- He treats us like children.
- His speech mannerism is like giving orders; very abrupt; and very impersonal.

- He tends to be short tempered, and sometimes uses foul language.
- His only concern is work; he does not care about our welfare.
- He wants us to work like robots.
- He is hesitant to teach us new skills.
- He sits with his feet up on the desk, with the bottom of his shoes facing us.
- He does not respect our culture and religion.

Surely, this is a case where *both* parties can use cultural orientation. Very few companies that I know of conduct orientation programs for their national Gulf employees. In one company that does that, nationals become familiar with Western values, beliefs, work habits and managerial styles, while the Western expatriates become acquainted with Arabian Gulf culture and management practices. Such programs usually lead to better communication and less misunderstanding between members of the two cultures.

On being an expatriate in the Gulf

For non-Arab expatriates, living and working in the Arabian Gulf could turn out to be anywhere from a disappointing, frustrating experience to an extremely rewarding, challenging one. The outcome, whether success or failure, depends for the most part on the cross-cultural training and orientation received by expatriates – before and after arrival in the host country. Interestingly enough, all expatriates whatever their nationalities will suffer from what is called "culture shock" when moving into a new culture. Culture shock will inevitably take place even for the seasoned well-traveled expatriate. It happened to my family and me when we moved, for the *second* time, to Greece after an absence of only four years! It also happened during the first time we resided in the Gulf (in Qatar) during the early 1980s.

Culture shock is the feeling of confusion followed by frustration or even depression that results from encountering different cultures. Culture shock is the "occupational hazard of living overseas", according to Kohls (2001). Orientation to the new culture can possibly reduce the harshness and duration of the culture shock. Incidentally, an expatriate returning to his or her country of origin after a prolonged period abroad will also suffer from the problems of what is called "re-entry transition" – re-learning the ropes and getting familiar with the "new" place!

To reduce culture shock, one of the first and most important tasks for expatriates would be to understand themselves and their own culture. Ironically, this is too often taken for granted or belittled. It is only by contrast with another culture that one is able to identify the specific or unusual characteristics of one's own culture. A better understanding of one's self brings out the crucial ingredients for success, namely:

- the ability to respect and tolerate different cultures
- avoidance of feeling of arrogance and sense of superiority
- avoidance of stereotyping
- having empathy and patience with unfamiliar people and situations
- being broad-minded and flexible
- being open – observing, listening, learning, and willing to experiment with new "foreign" situations and ideas.

Awareness of one's own culture is not sufficient, however. It has to be followed by a deeper understanding of the foreign culture – its history, religion, social structure, values and norms, and so on. The combination of these two types of cross-cultural orientation normally leads to better empathy with, and more tolerance to, foreign cultures.

> *Initially, foreigners may feel that Arabs are difficult to understand, that their behavior patterns are not logical. In fact, their behavior is quite comprehensible, even predictable. For the most part, it conforms to certain patterns which make Arabs consistent in their relations to other people.*
>
> It is important for the foreigner to be aware of the cultural patterns, to distinguish them from individual traits. *By becoming aware of patterns, one can achieve a better understanding of what to expect and thereby cope more easily (Author's emphasis).*
>
> (From *Understanding Arabs: A Guide for Westerners*, by Margaret (Omar) Nydell, 2002)

When an expatriate is unable to cope with the experience of living abroad, the typical reaction on the one extreme is to withdraw into a safe enclave surrounded by a circle of compatriots, or on the other extreme to "go native". Both reactions should be avoided. There is no harm if withdrawal is temporary and if it occurs infrequently; but complete withdrawal, or going native, is considered a failure. In both cases, the rich experiences of living in a different culture are missed and wasted, not to mention the negative effect on overall work performance. The expatriate and his family must enlarge their circle of friends and acquaintances to include several of the many nationalities living and working in the Gulf. Going native means adopting the habits of the host country, including some of the undesirable habits that the nationals themselves are trying to get rid of, such as low value of time, social visits during working hours, and so on.

An unfortunate mistake frequently made by expatriates is to equate the national employee's ability, intelligence, or potential with his fluency in the English language. I have come across many expatriate managers whose assessment of potential of national employees was influenced by the latter's ability to carry out social conversations in English.

Finally, there seem to be at least two general roles for expatriates. The first role expectation is to assist in the transfer of technology; and the second role is to act as a cultural bridge between the mother and host cultures. Transfer of technology means more than simply carrying out the job, or demonstrating the expertise for which expatriates are employed, or installation of high tech equipment and plants; it requires systematic coordination and cooperation with a view to training and developing the national workforce. In fact, more and more employment contracts and joint ventures stipulate the training of nationals. Therefore, both ability and willingness to train are becoming important criteria when recruiting expatriates or negotiating joint ventures.

The second role calls for expatriates, especially those at high levels in the organization, to be good representatives, or ambassadors, of their countries. Whether they know it or not, expatriates represent their countries and their cultures to members of the host country, portraying either a negative or positive reputation or image of their countries. Furthermore, expatriates, sometimes inadvertently, become teachers of their cultures and values to the inquisitive nationals of the host country. Of course, one hopes that only good and beneficial values are taught. Another role expectation for the expatriate is to become a student of the host culture. I feel very disappointed whenever I meet those few expatriates who have lived in the Gulf for several years, yet have very little knowledge of the Gulf's culture, religion or local customs. It is a lifetime opportunity to learn about other people, yet it is sometimes wasted. By the way, I would advise expatriates to learn only a few

Arabic phrases and words – for purposes of courtesy and showing respect rather than to conduct serious business or social conversations.

The question of accountability

No reflections on management would be complete without a brief discussion of accountability.

The question of individual and corporate accountability has been on my mind for many years, in fact ever since I was taught that people should be held accountable for results in their respective areas of authority and responsibility. I was convinced then, as I am now, that success in management (and in life) cannot be fully achieved if accountability is weak or absent. Unfortunately, I believe that more and more people are nowadays playing the "blame game": ducking personal responsibility, finding excuses, pointing fingers and attributing problems to "circumstances" or to others – rather than holding themselves accountable for their own behavior, actions or inaction, decisions or lack of decisions.

Even corporate accountability has taken a severe setback lately. As I write this chapter, the USA is going through a major crisis in corporate confidence in the aftermath of the scandals and wrongdoings at a number of companies such as Enron, Arthur Andersen, Tyco, Global Crossing, Xerox and WorldCom. As a result, there are loud calls for more integrity and transparency in business management, for trustworthy governance, and for renewed corporate accountability.

It is difficult, of course, to expect employees or teams working in an organization or institution to be held accountable if the top leadership itself is exempted from accountability. All too often, when things go wrong, "leaders" look for scapegoats or for "someone to hang"! This leadership attitude further encourages passing the buck, blaming others, and so on. And the vicious cycle goes on.

One definition of accountability that I like is:

> *An attitude of continually asking "what else can I do to rise above my circumstances and achieve the results I desire?" It is the process of "seeing it, owning it, solving it, and doing it." It requires a level of ownership that includes making, keeping, and proactively answering for personal commitments. It is a perspective that embraces both current and future efforts rather than reactive and historical explanations.*

(Connors et al., 1994)

Making excuses is as bad as pointing fingers. Here is a list of ten excuses used by people when explaining failure:

1 *It's not my job.*
2 *I didn't know you needed it right away.*
3 *That's the way we've always done it.*
4 *No one told me what to do.*
5 *I didn't know.*
6 *I forgot.*
7 *I was too busy to do it.*
8 *I am waiting for approval.*
9 *I told someone else to take care of it.*
10 *My people dropped the ball.*

(Adapted from *The Oz Principle*, Connors et al., 1994).

No one should be encouraged to use excuses to duck responsibility. Check to see if you are occasionally using excuses for failures to perform. If so, some intense soul-searching and critical self-analysis is called for. In addition, if your children or direct subordinates are using such excuses, then some serious discussions with them should take place. Without accountability, all parties involved will suffer in both the long and short run.

Lastly, there is one dark side of accountability; namely, taking credit for the successes of others, whether individual or team successes. Managers who do that should recognize that their subordinates or colleagues would ultimately lose any respect they may have had for them, not to mention the negative effect that this type of action will have on morale and productivity.

Let me end this brief section with an old, but wise, saying, "*Success has a thousand fathers, but failure is an orphan.*" Think about it; there is more than one way to interpret this old saying!

A closing comment

"It's tough in the Gulf" is a slogan that was once printed on T-shirts, and was frequently discussed by expatriates in social gatherings. The Gulf was indeed tough twenty or thirty years ago; difficult living conditions and lack of convenient facilities made the region a harsh area, not to mention the very hot summer weather. In fact, some companies paid hardship allowances for living and working in most parts of the Gulf. Today, things have changed drastically; from air conditioning everywhere, inexpensive domestic and professional services, comfortable roads and highways, Internet cafés, hotels and fancy restaurants, to modern indoor shopping malls – in short, conveniences everywhere.

However, I believe that the Gulf is still "tough" in other ways. For the Gulf Arab, workplace competition is becoming very intense and the easy days are distant memories. Conducting business or managing people are becoming more demanding and stressful. Nowadays, only the competent and highly motivated will be successful. Governments are becoming less generous with social benefits and welfare; and there are plans for privatization of public companies and a reduction in subsidies for some basic commodities, utilities, and so forth. Continuing education, training, self-development, and hard work are not a luxury anymore.

For expatriate employees working for local organizations, the greatest threat is nationalization (localization) and consequent loss of jobs. Alcohol is not allowed in two of the six GCC countries, and women cannot drive in one of them.

For expatriates working for multinational companies, or for those conducting business in the Gulf, tougher competition and lower margins are the order of the day, and it seems that this will continue for the near future.

Overall, it's not really that tough in the Gulf any more. It is a good place to live and work.

Note

It was the anthropologist Carleton S. Coon, in reference to the Middle East, who coined the term mosaic; see his book *Caravan: The Story of the Middle East*, revised edition (1958). Others have also used the mosaic metaphor when discussing the region.

> *The Middle East comprises an intricately complex mosaic of individuals who form groups based on kinship, nationality, religion, geographic location, profession, and political ideology. . . . The overall social structure might best be viewed as a divided grid or creased mosaic in which the intricate web of groups is partially partitioned by class lines.*

Chapter Six

The helicopter

Creative problem solving and decision making

A problem well stated is a problem half solved.

(Charles Kettering)

If a man takes no thought about what is distant, he will find sorrow near at hand.

(Confucius)

Problems cannot be solved by the same level of thinking that created them.

(Albert Einstein)

This chapter is about using the *helicopter view* in creative problem solving and decision making. It would be difficult to adequately cover the subject of problem solving and decision making in one chapter; indeed, there are many publications dedicated to this subject. The aim here is to highlight the importance of the helicopter in the thinking process.

I have long believed that problems are golden opportunities for improvement, in the same way many organizations nowadays view customer complaints as gifts.

We have no problems – every problem is an opportunity in disguise.

This phrase is from a stimulating book entitled *The Creative Gap* by Simon Majaro (1988). He wrote: "... as a first step try to approach the problem-solving process with a positive mind. Whether you are a businessperson, a civil servant, a politician or an ordinary citizen, remember that solving problems must not be a trauma. It is a challenge which the optimist is more likely to solve than the pessimist." I fully endorse Majaro's view; and would add that, for me as for many people, solving problems using creative tools and techniques can be a lot of fun, just like solving puzzles.

How, you may ask, can we turn a problem that is on the verge of becoming a crisis into an opportunity or a challenge? Especially if the problem is so serious that the roof seems to be collapsing on your head, or the consequences appear to be emotionally traumatic or financially devastating? How can we become optimists, and perhaps more creative?

The helicopter view is a simple, yet powerful concept that, I believe, holds the key to these questions. This is a concept that over the years has helped me, my family, business colleagues, and clients, avoid the main perils of problem solving: losing sight of the big picture, rushing to a wrong solution or in the wrong direction, and emotionally over-reacting.

The helicopter view refers to the ability to rise above the specifics of a situation and perceive it in its overall environment. It is the ability to see the forest for the trees, to see the total situation and how it relates to the larger context – seeing the big picture.

The helicopter concept is not new, it was coined last century by a large international organization. In their search for traits or factors common to their own successful managers and executives, they found that the helicopter view was the one factor most common among those executives. In fact, some organizations today have included this ability (competency) in their performance appraisal and performance management schemes. Some call it "peripheral vision" or "breadth of vision" or "clarity of purpose" or "power of anticipation".

Developing the helicopter view requires constant practice – it is an ongoing discipline, not one that can be left dormant and tapped at will in times of crisis. I started teaching the helicopter view to our three daughters while they were in their early teens. My wife and I did not want to send them far off to university before providing them with the tools, the methods and the thinking processes required to solve problems or to overcome crises. Thus, at a young age, whenever they faced a problem or a crisis, we would "walk" through the steps of problem solving, always starting with the helicopter view. Even today, we remind ourselves to "take the helicopter first" before going through the next steps of problem solving.

In our creative problem-solving seminars, we encourage managers to begin their analysis with a statement of what the problem looks like when viewed from a helicopter. Similarly, executives attending our strategic thinking and planning workshops are introduced to the concept. The simplicity of using the helicopter appeals to many managers. The helicopter metaphor is also memorable, and it is a great pleasure to hear occasionally from a manager who attended our seminars years ago saying: "I am still using the helicopter!" In fact, at the end of two recent in-company seminars the participants went out and bought one toy model helicopter for each manager to keep on their desk. My own office has a variety of model helicopters; I take one of the lighter ones with me whenever conducting problem-solving or strategy seminars!

The helicopter view

A person or a management team confronting a problem/crisis, or when required to formulate a strategy, can learn how to use the helicopter in three easy steps:

First, distance yourself mentally (and physically if needed) from the present situation. It is like riding up in a helicopter when lost in a forest, where only then can one see the dimensions of the forest or one's current location. It is also like stepping back from a large painting or a map in order to see the whole picture. This is similar to "zooming out" when looking through the lens of a camera. In short, looking at the current problem or crisis from a broader, bird's eye view. Try applying this distancing on the puzzle box below.

Find the missing total.

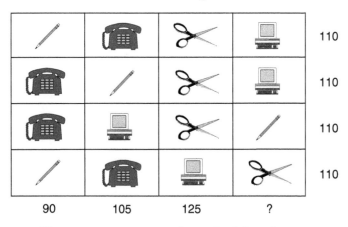

The answer appears at the end of this chapter.

When up in the helicopter, it becomes much clearer that the main problem is usually made up of a set of smaller inter-related problems, some long-term and others short-term. The relationships between the various problems become clearer, exactly the opposite of looking at a problem with a narrow, tunnel vision. As a result, prioritizing these smaller problems in terms of their importance and urgency will be much easier.

In the case of a crisis, the enormity of the situation becomes much less and ceases to be a panic-stricken "it's the end of the world" feeling. Instead, a calmer, more relaxed state of mind takes over, thereby avoiding the common pitfall of jumping to wrong conclusions or solutions because of "perceived" pressure and stress.

Second, describe today's current problem or crisis as though you were looking at it three, five or ten years from now. Assume that the person facing the crisis is currently 30 years old, ask him or her how they would describe the current crisis five years hence, or when 35 years old. The immediate reaction is usually a smile, followed by something like, "I'd probably have forgotten all about it!" Projecting oneself into the future makes the current problem seem much smaller and more manageable, rather than overwhelming.

Take a moment to reflect upon a serious problem or a crisis you have faced three or five years ago. At that very moment in time you probably thought that the world was collapsing around you. Looking back, how do you remember it today? From a historic perspective, yesterday's crises are seen as distant memories, and, if a person is lucky and wise, as learning experiences.

In our strategic thinking seminars, we start by asking managers to write down their current age, as well as their age ten years from now (it always seems easier to get them thinking of the future when it is personalized). Then we ask them to describe their business as of the second date, "What will your industry look like in ten years? What about your competitors? What about changes in governmental legislation, politics, demography, technology?" and so on. The next step is to ask them, "What will you do, if such changes happen?" Alternative scenarios for the future are then articulated, and strategies drawn around them.

These scenarios are designed to encourage managers to continuously question their assumptions and reorganize their mental maps of the real world. More importantly, it encourages managers to continue to learn as they make decisions about the future, a learning process that was described in *The Living Company* (de Geus, 1999). For more about strategic thinking and planning, see Chapter 7, The bridge.

Third, once the present and the future are put in perspective, we can focus on the future direction, using the helicopter repeatedly to ensure that we are staying on the right path. Having isolated the most important/urgent priority problems, the helicopter descends for a closer look at the details. The advantages of using the helicopter are in its ability to go vertically up and down, zooming in and out so as not to lose sight of the significant details.

Thus, the helicopter view can and should be used *at any stage* in the problem solving or strategy formulation processes. These up and down movements ensure that we stay on the right course and avoid focusing so closely on the trees.

For example, suppose that there is a crisis of late delivery for a valued customer. Reacting narrowly to what might be a one-off problem (sales delivery in this case) while paying little attention to other inter-related issues of manufacturing, supply chain or quality may lead to disastrous long-term results. In other words, one can run the danger of solving a specific problem while unknowingly creating or overlooking other much more serious ones. Using the helicopter view ensures that a long-term, holistic approach is used in solving complex and inter-related problems.

There is an old story of three stonecutters who were asked what they were doing.

> *The first replied:* "I am making a living."
> *The second said:* "I am doing the best job of stonecutting in the entire country."
> *The third one looked up with a gleam in his eyes and said:* "I am building a mansion."

> *If these three were managers, then the third is a true manager; he relates his work to the needs of the whole activity. The second loses sight of the whole and tends to divert his vision and efforts from the goals of the organization. He is the specialist who loses himself in his own specialty and forgets that it is only a part of the whole. The first stonecutter, of course, is the hard worker who is likely to give a "fair day's work for a fair day's pay".*

Creativity in problem solving

My first encounter with a well-structured and systematic approach to problem solving came in the early 1970s when attending an in-company course in California. It was based on the book *The Rational Manager* by Charles Kepner and Benjamin Tregoe (1965). The course had a tremendous impact on my thinking and future work. After completing it, I immediately shared the techniques with my associates at work.

The more we used the Kepner-Tregoe system the more curious I became about the role of creativity in problem solving. The search for creativity tools and methods led me to various excellent problem-solving concepts developed by Kaoru Ishikawa, Vilfredo Pareto, Alex Osborn, Edward de Bono, to name a few. Additionally, I continue to follow the ongoing research on the right and left hemispheres of the brain, and how they relate to problem solving.

Creativity, it seems, is greatly influenced by child upbringing. Well-meaning parents discourage, and sometimes punish, the inquisitive behavior and creative thinking of their children through inappropriate attempts at keeping them "well behaved" and disciplined. The child's exploration of objects and ideas, for example, are met with punitive responses or ridicule, mostly unintentional. I am sure that most of you have seen living rooms full of expensive ornaments and breakable knick-knacks that are left within reach of the child; and have observed the young parents' reaction to their child's curiosity and natural desire to explore and touch. The advice given to such parents is to remove or place higher such objects (which are usually meant to impress friends or family) and replace them for the time being with toys which the child can safely play with, and which satisfy his or her inquisitiveness and need for learning.

The situation is often further exacerbated by teachers and professors who over-emphasize learning "by the book", "rational" thinking, and following "acceptable" norms of behavior at the expense of creative thinking and innovation.

And finally when the individual joins a "typical" organization, whatever creativity he or she retained will be further stifled by the organization's rules, regulations and procedures – not to mention the boss or peers, if the person is really unlucky.

The main enemies of creativity are criticism and negative thinking. Hence, during brainstorming sessions newly suggested ideas are not evaluated or criticized immediately. One of Edward de Bono's six thinking hats is the "negative" black hat, an important and useful thinking hat, but one that is perhaps over-used, and certainly one that should not be worn too early during creative thinking sessions. As de Bono says in his book *Serious Creativity* (1992): "It is easy to kill creative ideas with early negativity."

How many cubes do you *see* in this figure?

A quick look at the above shape shows six cubes. If you mentally flip your perspective so you view the cubes as if from below, rather than from above, you can see seven cubes and parts of several others. The fact is that you can mentally change the orientation of the cubes at will. However, nothing changes in the illustration – you only change your perspective. (To help you see the seven cubes, rotate the page!)

Creativity is a skill that can be learned as well as an attitude to be acquired. How can we regain some of the creativity we all had as children? Is the situation hopeless? Definitely not! I am not sure who said, "The brain is like a muscle, if you don't use it, you'll lose it" – it makes a lot of sense. Clearly re-learning creative thinking, and practicing it on a continuous basis, may be the answer for many individuals. To put it simply: since creativity is found in all of us (with most experts agreeing that it is a combination of genetics and environment), it is in a way similar to our ability to walk and run. With training and exercise we can all improve, some could become faster runners, others will become marathon runners and a few could make it to the Olympics!

A recent search on Amazon.com showed that there are about 1700 books on creativity. The most comprehensive review of the subject, however, is found in the Handbook of Creativity, edited by R. Sternberg (1999). This rather academic review contains 22 chapters (460 pages) covering the history, research, and theories of creativity.

Here are two quick puzzles

1 Continue and explain the following letters progression:

A   E F   H I   ....
———————————————————————————————
B C D   G   J   ....

2 Continue and explain the following numeric progression:

3 1 2 8 3 1 3 0 ....

Answers appear at the end of this chapter.

Problem solving and decision making

The traditional and most widely accepted steps of problem solving are summarized as follows:

1 define the problem
2 analyze potential causes
3 generate alternative solutions
4 select the best solution
5 develop action and contingency plans
6 implement and evaluate progress.

Many experts and writers on this subject agree that it would be better to include both the *rational* and the *creative* aspects of thinking in the processes of problem solving and decision making. If that is the case, it is sensible to integrate a variety of creative techniques into the process. And that's precisely what we, at Meirc, did when designing our Problem Solving and Decision Making course. Drawing heavily from the works of various writers, we combined the rational thinking approach (Kepner and Tregoe, 1965) with the creative techniques of Ishikawa (1985), Pareto, Osborn (1963) and de Bono (1992). Additionally, we introduced the helicopter view at the start and in the middle of the problem-solving thinking process; in fact, we encourage using it at any time when a person or a team digresses or is stuck.

Here are the steps we use for problem solving and decision making. The reader will immediately notice that they are in line with Kepner and Tregoe's approach, shown on the right:

		Kepner and Tregoe's (1965) approach
The helicopter view The deviation diagram Ishikawa's fishbone diagram Brainstorming Pareto analysis (80–20 principle)	→	Situational appraisal and Problem analysis (PA)
The helicopter view Objectives Brainstorming de Bono's Six Thinking Hats The How-How? diagram	→	Decision analysis (DA)
Implementation plan Preventive actions Contingency plans Evaluating and measuring progress/KPIs	→	Potential problem analysis (PPA)

Here is a simple case study from a business setting to illustrate the above problem-solving steps:

The case of Nader

Nader has worked the last ten years for Union Contractors, a large and growing engineering company that provides complete engineering, construction, and procurement services for large industrial projects. His service with the firm has been a story of success, until recently. He came to the company directly from the University of Texas where he received a very good advanced technical education. During his early years, he did very well as a project engineer, showing high potential for advancement. His success was due to his attention to the needs of the projects, his hard work, and his habit of carefully planning his activities.

As a result, Nader was rapidly promoted until he reached the position of Assistant Area Project Manager, a post that he held for some time. During his entire career, Nader had always worked under the direction of Mr. Salem, a strong, aggressive, decisive and dictatorial individual. As Area Project Manager, Mr. Salem also had vast technical knowledge, wide knowledge of the industry and an ambition for himself and for the organization.

Mr. Salem, as he liked to be called, did not believe in delegating. Instead, he insisted on making all the decisions in his projects. He never forgave subordinates for their mistakes, regardless how small these mistakes were. His subordinates both feared and respected him and avoided any confrontations that might bring out his anger or disapproval.

Mr. Salem was effective as long as the projects were small and he could keep track of all the details. As projects grew in scope and size, his weaknesses began to show. When Union Contractors were awarded a very large two-year project, Mr. Salem had only spent a few weeks on the project before he fell seriously ill. The pressures of the job, as well as top management, had finally convinced him that retirement was his best decision.

During the search for a successor to Mr. Salem, management looked favorably toward Nader. He had already been given the post of Acting Area Project Manager for the interim period and everyone was optimistic in his abilities to meet the challenge. As time went on, however, he became very slow to make decisions, which finally led top management to decide, "He wasn't ready". Instead, the job went to another manager, Ramsey, who had just completed a very successful large project elsewhere in the country.

Upon assuming his new position, Ramsey looked to his assistant, Nader, to make some of the decisions and provide the leadership necessary for certain phases of the construction. However, over a period of several months he began to worry about Nader's slow approach to making decisions.

After speaking with Nader about this difficulty, Ramsey found that Nader reasoned brilliantly in analyzing problems that arose on site, and that his technical skills coupled with his detailed knowledge of the project were most helpful. But when it came to making decisions to meet the agreed time schedules, he was hesitant to take the plunge. Department heads complained that they failed to get clear, prompt directives and support.

At first, Ramsey hoped that Nader's performance would improve. He began to apply pressure into forcing more rapid decisions or action. Yet he found that Nader always had an excuse; either more facts were needed, or he was not receiving proper support from his subordinates, or the plans were not complete and every part had to fit perfectly together before it would be safe to go ahead and implement it. By the end of the first year, Ramsey was dissatisfied with Nader's performance and felt that some change was finally needed.

About this time, Ramsey was negotiating with the client, and it seemed that new changes and additional demands by the client would require the setting up of a separate Planning Department. In choosing a person to head the new department, Ramsey saw an opportunity to move Nader out of his present position where his indecisiveness was becoming a serious handicap. Ramsey knew that the results of the work would not be tough decisions, but mostly recommendations of plans and programs, or reports on projects already in progress.

Nader threw himself whole-heartedly into the work of organizing his new department, although it was a quickly assembled team from various other units. Within a few months, however, other department heads began to complain bitterly that they "couldn't get anything out of Nader's group". When Ramsey discussed the problem with Nader, he received his usual explanations. His people were untrained for the work. They did not understand all the implications of the planning process. The job of training them and forming a good working team was proving more difficult than Nader had expected. Ramsey urged Nader to use the existing software to list and prioritize the various projects he must plan, to estimate the time needed for each and to prepare time and cost schedules in the form of charts, copies of which he would receive. Nader expressed enthusiasm for this idea, but some way or other was too busy to implement it.

Facing mounting complaints, the Area General Manager and Ramsey are at a loss as to what they should do about Nader. They are impressed by the fact he has one of the best brains in the company. They see in his technical knowledge a valuable asset that the company cannot afford to lose. He seems worth saving if it can be done. However, something has to be done about Nader – and fast.

Commentary
At first glance, the solution to this fictional case study seems obvious: Since Nader does not seem to have been properly prepared for a managerial job, Union Contractors must quickly train Nader, especially on decision making. If after a while this approach fails, then Nader ought to be moved sideways or out.

What if we use the problem-solving steps outlined earlier? Will our solution be the same?

Suggested solution
Looking at this case from a helicopter view reveals several inter-related problems at three levels: organizational, departmental

and individual. Additionally, these problems are both short- and long-term in nature as shown.

Short-term (at the individual and departmental levels):
(a) Nader is clearly ineffective as manager of the new Planning Department.
(b) The performance of other departments is suffering, producing a negative impact on the company's performance.

Long-term (at the organizational level):
(a) It seems that there is a lack of a succession planning system, which can normally be used to select replacements for sudden or unplanned departures of key managers.
(b) There seems to be no systematic career development plans that identify and track high potential employees, or a system that designs, implements and monitors developmental plans for these high flyers.
(c) The performance appraisal system at Union Contractors appears to be ineffective since it allowed managers like Salem to get away for a long time with serious managerial shortcomings and practices.
(d) In the longer run, the reputation of Union Contractors as a preferred employer could be at risk. As a growing company, they may not be able to attract new talent if similar incidents continue to recur.

In fact, looking at this case study from the helicopter view gives management a golden opportunity to address a serious shortcoming in their human resources function, namely, the lack of succession planning and career development systems. They should be glad that this problem occurred now before it repeats in other departments or in other regional divisions of the company. Indeed, as mentioned at the beginning of this chapter, problems should often be viewed as opportunities in disguise!

Faced with these short and long-term problems, top management should first prioritize the problems according to urgency and importance. Let us suppose the short-term problem of what to do with Nader is chosen.

The deviation diagram, Figure 6.1, shows that this problem began a long time ago when Nader started reporting to Salem, whose autocratic style and lack of delegation probably contributed to Nader's fear of making decisions. The situation worsened when Ramsey threw Nader in the deep end as a department manager without proper training or support.

Using the brainstorming technique and the Ishikawa fishbone diagram, several root causes were identified, as shown in the fishbone diagram, Figure 6.2.

Incidentally, my experience using this simple and visual fishbone diagram has shown that it has several benefits:

(a) It encourages an individual (or members of the team) to study every angle of a problem before making a hasty decision as to what are the main root causes.

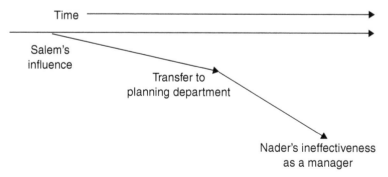

Figure 6.1 The deviation diagram

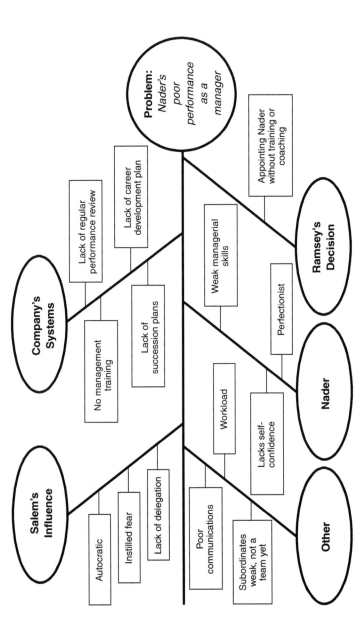

Figure 6.2 Fishbone diagram for the case of Nader

(b) It helps to show the inter-relationships between parts of the problem, and the relative importance of each part.
(c) It helps people to avoid concentrating all their attention on one cause or one part of the problem, thus offering a total approach perspective – a helicopter view.
(d) It prevents anyone from rushing into half-cooked solutions.

Once the Ishikawa diagram is fully completed, and the sub-causes examined in some depth, one must decide which of the causes are contributing the most to the problem. The weight or importance assigned to each of the causes is normally determined by the data available, or by using one's experience and judgment. Using the 80–20 Pareto principle, one can say that about 80 per cent of the problem is due to 20 per cent of the causes. That is, only two or three of the causes shown on the fishbone diagram have contributed 80 per cent of the problem. The Pareto principle was named after the Italian economist Vilfredo Pareto who discovered the 80–20 principle in 1897. One hundred years later, Richard Koch wrote the first-ever published book about the Pareto principle (*The 80/20 Principle*, Koch, 1998). In it, he explains how this principle could be profitably applied in nearly all aspects of life and business. Koch states, "The *minority* of causes, inputs, or efforts usually lead to a *majority* of results, outputs, or rewards" (emphasis added).

Returning to Nader's case, three main causes seem to have led to Nader's poor performance as a manager: (Cause 1) lack of training and career development plan; (Cause 2) Salem's influence that resulted in Nader's fear of making decisions; and (Cause 3) Ramsey's last decision to move Nader to a newly formed department. Therefore, the Pareto 80–20 chart for Nader's case would look like Figure 6.3.

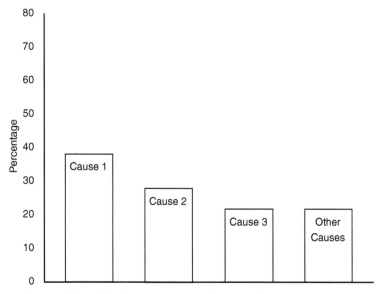

Figure 6.3   The Pareto 80–20 chart for the case of Nader

A typical (Pareto) pattern will show that 80 per cent of outputs result from 20 per cent of inputs; that 80 per cent of consequences flow from 20 per cent of causes; or that 80 per cent of results come from 20 per cent of effort.

(From *The 80/20 Principle*, Richard Koch, 1998)

The How-How? diagram, Figure 6.4, can now be used to identify the specific steps that should be taken to achieve the desired objective or solution. In this case, the short-term objective is to improve Nader's managerial competencies, especially his decision-making skills while the longer-term objectives are to find solutions to each of the several organizational level problems mentioned earlier.

The How-How? diagram has many advantages. It allows team members to generate creative alternatives and solutions without

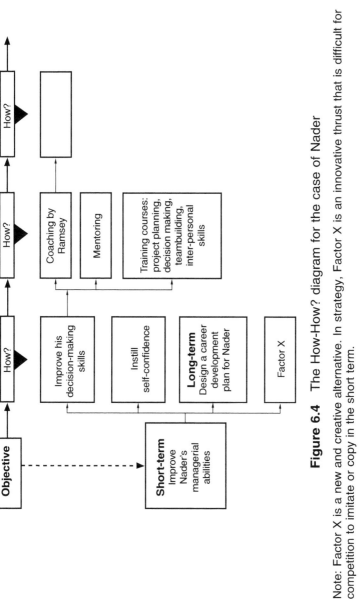

Figure 6.4 The How-How? diagram for the case of Nader

Note: Factor X is a new and creative alternative. In strategy, Factor X is an innovative thrust that is difficult for competition to imitate or copy in the short term.

losing sight of the overall objective(s) that is stated in the head of the How-How? diagram. It encourages members to ask repeatedly "How else?" can this problem be solved. Edward de Bono's thinking hats are particularly useful during these discussions, especially the green hat (for generation of ideas and alternatives), to be followed by the yellow hat (positive thinking/benefits and evaluation of the ideas), and then the black hat (negative thinking and evaluation).

During our seminars and workshops, groups working on more complex problems can generate a large number of flip chart sheets of How-How? diagrams posted around the walls of the room for all to see. When fully completed, if the Ishikawa diagram looks like a large fish, the How-How? diagrams will certainly look like a large octopus!

From time to time, we also urge group members to stand back, get into the helicopter, and ask, "Are we going in the right direction?" and, "What are the long-term implications of doing this or that?"

Returning to our case study, Ramsey should now implement an action plan with the aim of coaching Nader on decision making. In the beginning, the coaching will be frequent and intensive, perhaps on a weekly basis. Ramsey should assist Nader in making hard and fast decisions on all pending matters. Ramsey may have to take the decisions himself at first, while explaining his rationale, pointing out the nuances between what is urgent, and what is important. With time, Ramsey will lessen his input while still reviewing the decisions made by Nader, thus gradually delegating more of the decisions that in fact belong to Nader. It is like teaching someone how to swim, where supervision gradually decreases as skills and confidence increase.

In addition, a mentor should be assigned to Nader in order to counsel, advise and help him during this crucial period. Nader will also be attending seminars on project planning, decision-making techniques, team-building, and inter-personal skills. All these actions may result in increased self-confidence and may develop managerial skills, which Nader urgently needs. Of course, continuous follow up and monitoring of Nader's progress is essential, especially during the early period of this program.

What can go wrong? Well, Nader may not improve even after all the managerial training and coaching; in which case another decision will have to be made regarding his career with Union Contractors. Either he is moved to a meaningful technical (non-managerial) position within the firm, or, as a last resort, he is helped to find a job elsewhere.

However, the main, and more serious, long-term problem remains, which is how to avoid similar situations from occurring in the future. How can we prevent similar cases arising again? How can we prevent the future "Salems of this world" from inflicting damage on their subordinates? In this instance, the human resources department in Union Contractors will require a series of new systems and initiatives. For example, there is an immediate need for an integrated performance management system; such a system should link organizational-level core competencies with other human resources functions: recruitment and selection, performance appraisal, compensation and rewards, identification of high potential employees, career development, and training. Of course, top management commitment, involvement, and active support will be required to make these systems work effectively.

A closing comment

The helicopter view, the deviation diagram, Ishikawa's fishbone, Pareto's 80–20 chart, de Bono's six thinking hats, and the How-

How? method are all tools that could be used in creative problem solving and decision making. All of them share a common advantage: they are easy to use and they invoke the visual senses. Over the years, I have found that most people grasp and remember concepts or methods much better if they are visual. Perhaps the Chinese proverb says it well, "A picture is worth a thousand words"!

Answer to "Find the Missing Total"

There are two ways to find the right answer. One is to calculate the value of each item in the grid and find that the missing total is 120.

Another way to find the missing total is to get into the helicopter and look at the total figure, not at the items in the grid. Cover the shaded items. Clearly, if the value of the items is 110 + 110 + 110 + 110 = 440 when adding the numbers vertically, then surely their total will be the same if added horizontally; hence 90 + 105 + 125 = 320 which is then subtracted from the grand total of 440 giving us: 440 − 320 = 120. The first method is like looking at the individual trees, the second looks at the whole forest! Much easier, isn't it?

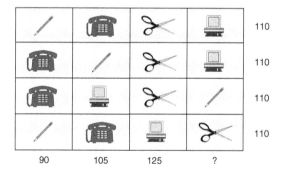

Answers to the two puzzles

1 The letters in the top have straight lines only; those at the bottom have curves.
2 The numbers indicate the number of days in the months. Thus, January = 31, February = 28, March = 31, and so on.

Chapter Seven

The bridge

Strategic thinking and retirement planning

Chance favors the prepared mind.

(Louis Pasteur)

To look backward for a while is to refresh the eye, to restore it, and to render it more fit for its prime function of looking forward.

(Margaret F Barber)

All men can see the tactics whereby I conquer, but what none can see is the strategy out of which great victory is evolved.

(Sun-Tzu, Chinese Military Strategist, 4th century BC)

"Competition is getting much tougher". "Our competitors are becoming more ruthless!" "It's getting more difficult to see into the future". We are hearing these outcries more and more. Well, are we really surprised? As globalization, deregulation, or privatization become more of a reality, and as world economies continue to experience sharp turns and swings, competition will certainly turn into a global hyper-competition. Old competitors as well as new entrants will use unrelenting maneuvers and clever tactics to gain market share, or to create new markets with innovative products and services.

To survive, prosper and grow, large and small organizations are increasingly turning to strategy and strategic management. However, what exactly is strategy? There are several schools of thought (and many gurus) on strategy each claiming to be more right than the other. For a thorough review and excellent critique of the strategy field, I refer you to the book by Henry Mintzberg *et al.*, *Strategy Safari: A Guided Tour through the Wilds of Strategic Management* (1998), where they reviewed and critiqued ten approaches to strategic management.

Mintzberg *et al.* began their book, *Strategy Safari* (1998), with the often referred to fable of the six blind men and the elephant. This introductory statement followed the fable:

> *We are the blind people and strategy formation is our elephant. Since no one has had the vision to see the entire beast, everyone has grabbed hold of some part or other and 'railed on in utter ignorance' about the rest. We certainly do not get an elephant by adding up its parts. An elephant is more than that. Yet to comprehend the whole we also need to understand the parts.*

Mintzberg *et al.* also suggested five definitions of strategy – the 5 Ps, as they called them:

1 "*Strategy is a plan* – a direction, a course of action into the future, a path to get from here to there." (Looking ahead.)
2 "*Strategy is a pattern*, that is, consistency in behavior over time." (Looking at past behavior.)

3 "*Strategy is a position*, namely the locating of particular products in particular markets." (Looking at where the product meets the customer, and looking out to the external market place.)
4 "*Strategy is a perspective*, namely an organization's fundamental way of doing things the McDonald's way", or the HP way, the Pepsi way, and so on. (Looking inside the organization, and looking up to the vision of the enterprise.)
5 "*Strategy is a ploy*, that is, a specific 'maneuver' intended to outwit an opponent or competitor."

A good strategy, I believe, should encompass most, if not all, these definitions. Moreover, strategy formation should be a flexible, incremental and continuous process; that is, an organization should be able to change and adapt its strategy in line with the ever-changing conditions within the organization and in the outside world. Professor Ken Simmonds of London Business School once compared strategic processes with playing a Monopoly game: you are constantly observing the opponents' moves, evaluating your own and your opponents' situation, and re-formulating your next strategy or tactics. This is of course feasible, as long as the organization's core values and core purpose do not change dramatically.

Finally, it is clear that strategic *thinking* has displaced strategic planning as the jumping board, or the starting point, of developing strategies; Mintzberg argued in his (1993) book, *The Rise and Fall of Strategic Planning*, that strategic planning sometimes gets in the way of strategic thinking. The former has always been about "analysis" while the latter, in contrast, is about "synthesis". Strategic thinking also involves intuition and creativity. According to Kenichi Ohmae (1982), some of the secrets of strategic vision are:

- a broader view, instead of tunnel vision
- strategic and creative thinking, instead of inflexible thinking
- keeping details in perspective, instead of the time-consuming obsession with details, or the often referred to "paralysis by analysis".

This chapter is not about developing strategies, a subject that requires several volumes to cover in any depth, and a field still waiting for synthesis. Instead, this chapter introduces *the bridge,* a tool used by senior and line managers to start the *process* of thinking strategically. Building the bridge is the first critical step of drafting a tentative, broad and future-oriented strategy. Later, managers throughout the organization can work the finer details and develop the implementation plans.

The bridge concept incorporates most, if not all, the definitions of strategy suggested by Mintzberg *et al.* If strategy is a journey to the future, the bridge is the direction and the path to get from the present to the future. The bridge asks managers to position their products or services based on market and environmental analysis, keeping in mind past behavior. And at the same time, building it relies heavily on the vision statement and takes into account corporate values to reflect the interests of the stakeholders.

Incidentally, the bridge is also a *visual tool* which seminar and workshop participants find easier to remember and understand. (We found out that building a bridge is more exciting and creative than drawing strategy diagrams or process-maps; it hints at a bit of design, engineering, challenge, risk, and even an expression of art!)

Building the bridge

There are *four* phases to building the strategy bridge:

Phase 1: The future
Phase 2: The past, the present, and future scenarios
Phase 3: The values
Phase 4: The scorecard

However, a note of caution at the outset: these phases are not carried out in a neat consequential order; for example, one starts working on phase one, moves to phase two, and then returns to phase one again, and so forth. Furthermore, the strategy that emerges out of the bridge building is viewed by the organization as a broad and *flexible* blueprint that is altered and modified during implementation as future events unfold. Figure 7.1 represents the bridge building phases.

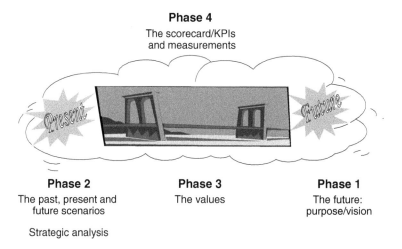

Figure 7.1   Four phases to building the strategy bridge

Phase 1: the future

This phase starts with an initial attempt at articulating the organization's statement of purpose, vision or mission. If one already exists, then a brief re-visit is necessary to ensure that the statement is still valid or realistic.

James Collins and Jerry Porras (1997) have provided one of the best definitions of vision that I have come across. They wrote:

> A *well-conceived vision consists of two major components –* core ideology *and an* envisioned future . . . *(emphasis by the two authors). A good vision builds on the interplay between these complementary yin-and-yang forces: it defines "what we stand for and why we exist" that does not change (the core ideology) and sets forth "what we aspire to become, to achieve, to create" that will require significant change and progress to attain (the envisioned future).*
>
> *To pursue the vision means to create organizational and strategic alignment to preserve the core ideology and stimulate progress toward the envisioned future. Alignment brings the vision to life, translating it from good intentions to concrete reality.*

Once the *core ideology* portion of a vision or purpose statement is either tentatively articulated, or re-visited if it already exists, we then move to Phase 2, keeping in mind that we shall return to Phase 1 to complete the *envisioned future* portion.

According to Collins and Porras (1997), core ideology itself consists of two distinct sub-components: core values and core purpose. One of the many examples given by the authors on core ideology is 3M.

3M
Core values:
- innovation; "thou shall not kill a new product idea"
- absolute integrity
- respect for individual initiative and personal growth
- tolerance for honest mistakes
- product quality and reliability.

Core purpose:
- "Our real business is solving problems" – (or, to solve unsolved problems innovatively).

The following are examples of statements of purpose for four other global companies:

Roche
Our aim is to discover, manufacture and market products and to provide services which address prevention, diagnosis and treatment of diseases, thus enhancing well-being and quality of life.

Sony
To experience the joy that comes from the advancement, application, and innovation of technology that benefits the general public.

Unilever
Our purpose in Unilever is to meet the everyday needs of people everywhere, to anticipate the aspirations of our consumers and customers, and to respond creatively and competitively with branded products and services which raise the quality of life.

Walt Disney
Our purpose is to make people happy.

To reiterate, according to Collins and Porras (1997), a vision is made partly of core ideology: (a) Core values (integrity, innovation, social responsibility, and so on); and (b) Core purpose – or the *raison d'être* of the organization. (Our purpose is to ... Usually it is an aim that is never totally reached because it is valid and continuous for decades to come; as can be seen from the purpose stated by each of the four companies). The other part of a well-conceived vision is envisioned future; we will return to it after completing Phase 2.

Throughout, I shall use examples taken from an assignment carried out by Meirc for a government agency. The fact that the government organization is a non-profit cost center, and seemingly without competition, made our assignment challenging and more interesting.

Not long ago, we facilitated strategy sessions for a police department using the bridge metaphor. After lively initial discussions, the top ranks of the organization agreed on the first draft of their vision or statement of purpose. It read: "The purpose of the [name of the police department] is to provide the community of [name of community] with world-class police services, security, and safety." Although Phase 1 was not completed, the group moved on to Phase 2. They will return later on to check if it is realistic, and to discuss the three pillars of the bridge: police services, safety and security.

Here are some mission and vision statements of six other police departments from around the world:

- The MISSION of the New York City Police Department is to enhance the quality of life in our City by working in partnership with the community and in accordance with constitutional rights to enforce the laws, preserve the peace, reduce fear, and provide for a safe environment.

- We are dedicated to delivering police services, in partnership with our communities, to keep Toronto the best and safest place to be.
- We, the members of the Glasgow Police Department, are dedicated to providing impartial law enforcement, community-oriented services and police protection in our City, while maintaining the highest ethical and professional standards.
- The mission of the Singapore Police Force is to uphold the law, maintain order and keep the peace in the Republic of Singapore. We do this by working in partnership with the community to protect life and property, prevent crimes and disorder, detect and apprehend offenders and preserve a sense of security.
- The purpose of the Delhi Police is to uphold the law fairly and firmly: To prevent crime; to pursue and bring to justice those who break the law; to keep the peace in partnership with the community; to protect, help and reassure the people; and to be seen to do all this with integrity, common sense and sound judgment.
- The mission of the Berlin Police Department is to provide community oriented law enforcement designed to protect life & property and maintain order, while assuring fair and equal treatment for all.

Source: Taken from the websites of the various police departments, 2002.

Phase 2: the past, the present, and future scenarios

This second phase involves external and internal strategic analysis, as well as a determination of future competitive advantages.

External analysis includes an examination of the significant elements external to the organization. The analysis should be brief and purposeful. One output of this analysis is an identification of opportunities and threats facing the organization, both potential and present. The aim is to discuss and visualize future scenarios taking into account past, present and likely future conditions. The participants in the strategy session are at all times encouraged to use the helicopter view in order to see the forest for the trees (see Chapter 6). Our presentation in this chapter is a very brief summary of strategic analysis; for more detailed and lengthy coverage of strategic analysis, I recommend David A. Aaker's, *Developing Business Strategies*, 6th edition (2001).

External analysis covers four components: customer analysis, competitive analysis, market analysis, and environmental analysis. Here, I shall list only a few sample questions on each component for discussion during strategy sessions.

- Who are our customers, and what are their unmet needs?
- Who are the competitors, and what are their strengths and weaknesses?
- What is the size of the market, and what are the significant market trends?
- What opportunities exist for possible acquisitions, strategic partnerships, demergers or spin-offs?
- What are the likely future needs of the community and other stakeholders?
- What are the most likely trends, threats and opportunities in each of the elements representing the external environment: demographic, cultural, economic, legislative, and technological? What will these external environments look like five or ten years from now? That is, what are the likely scenarios for each element of the external environment? And finally, what will we do, if such-and-such happens?

By reflecting on these questions, managers bring into their scenario analysis the past, present and future in one continuous cycle. Arie de Geus, in his book *The Living Company* (1999), says, "... scenarios served to change the ways in which managers saw and understood their world. Scenarios were designed to oblige managers to question their assumptions and recognize their inner mental maps of reality." According to Arie de Geus, managers engaged in planning for the future are continuously learning and, as he correctly maintains, that decision making itself is a learning activity; this type of thinking process will " ... encourage managers to continue to learn as they make decisions about the future".

At the police department that we worked with, participants considered scenarios on the future of their community, and the future role of the department in developing the community. Naturally, they focused more on the opportunities and threats stemming from the demographic, cultural, economic, legislative and technological environments, less on financial performance and competition. Interestingly, whenever I work with managers from government organizations their first reaction to the question, "Who is your competitor?", is to say, "We don't have any." On reflection, however, they identify two sources of competition: First, similar government organizations in the region or around the world (such as other police departments, public utilities, municipalities, and so on). Second, the organization *itself* is the competition, that is, there is a strong recognition and willingness to improve the current state of its operations and services. At the police department, we spent a large amount of time answering questions like these: What are our strengths and weaknesses? How can we become leaders in police services, security and safety? What do the best police departments in the world do?

> *Every morning in Africa, a gazelle wakes up. It knows that it must run faster than the fastest lion or it will be killed.*
> *Every morning a lion wakes up. It knows it must run faster than the slowest gazelle or it will starve to death.*
> *It doesn't matter whether you're a lion or a gazelle, or where in the world you work, in the modern business jungle when the sun comes up you'd better be running.*

Internal analysis takes a hard look at some strategy-related issues of the organization. It includes an examination of the organization's financial performance and constraints, customer loyalty and satisfaction, quality of products and services, and competencies of employees. It also examines past and current strategies, as well as organizational strengths and weaknesses. Finally, the analysis examines the core competencies needed to build or create competitive advantages for the future. Core competence describes the organization's capabilities – what the organization is particularly good at, for example, miniaturization at Sony.

In *Competing for the Future* (1994), Hamel and Prahalad argued that the new, smaller rivals were able to challenge "corporate giants" and industry leaders mainly because "the challengers had succeeded in creating entirely new forms of competitive advantage and in dramatically rewriting the rules of engagement". Managers of these new challengers were far more foresighted than other managers. They imagined products, services and even entire industries that did not exist and then created them.

According to Hamel and Prahalad,

Industry foresight helps managers answer three critical questions. First, what new types of customer benefit should we seek to provide in five, ten, or fifteen years? Second, what

new competencies will we need to build or acquire to offer those benefits to customers? And third, how will we need to reconfigure the customer interface over the next several years?
(Hamel and Prahalad, 1994)

They suggest that Motorola is a good example of a company with foresight. "Motorola dreams of a world in which telephone numbers will be assigned to people, rather than places; where small hand-held devices will allow people to stay in touch no matter where they are; and where the new communicators can deliver video images and data as well as voice signals." Organizations have first to understand and then develop unique core competencies (such as optical media, financial engineering, and miniaturization). To deliver customer benefits and value, Hamel and Prahalad (1994) suggest a blueprint ("strategic architecture") to provide guidance and broad plans on what the organization should be doing right now to prepare itself for the future.

The main aim of external and internal strategic analyses is to provide a deeper understanding of the past and present in order to envision the future direction, and to formulate the future competitive advantages of the organization. At this point, we are ready to do a *reality check* on the statement of purpose or vision drafted in Phase 1. Is the statement realistic and achievable? Does it align with the strategic analysis just completed in Phase 2? If not, then it may be necessary to re-articulate the statement of purpose before drafting the envisioned future. Just like building a real bridge, one works on both ends simultaneously: the future (Phase 1), and the past, present and future scenarios (Phase 2).

At this point in the process, strategic alternatives are identified. Using the How-How? method, which was described earlier in Chapter 6, the management group selects short- and long-term corporate and departmental objectives/goals. These corporate objectives are later translated into concrete action plans and budgets for eventual implementation.

Five simple questions brought strategic thinking to life for me:

- *What is the detailed global position of your business and that of your competitors: market shares, strengths by product line, and by region today?*
- *What actions have your competitors taken in the past two years that have changed the competitive landscape?*
- *What have you done in the last two years to alter that landscape?*
- *What are you most afraid your competitors might do in the next two years to change the landscape?*
- *What are you going to do in the next two years to leapfrog any of their moves?*

(Jack Welch on strategic thinking, *Jack: Straight from the Gut*, 2001)

Back to our example of the police department, based on the strategic analysis, the executive group decided that their vision statement is indeed realistic and achievable. To repeat, their vision statement read: "The purpose of the [name of the police department] is to provide the community of [name of community] with world-class police services, security, and safety." Now, the group moves to the envisioned future, namely, what concrete actions are required to become world-class in the three areas: police services, security, and safety. These three areas become the pillars that support the bridge.

Three teams, representing three divisions, were formed to work on each area. Using the How-How? method, each team recommended broad strategies and action plans for each divisional/organizational objective. Later on, line and staff people throughout the police department could work the finer details of the strategies, develop implementation plans, and prepare capital and operating budgets, and so on.

The group was convinced that the police department would have to utilize, among other things, leading-edge technology in order to achieve the three organizational objectives: excellence in police services, security and safety. The group discussed and agreed a large number of initiatives, most of which were eventually implemented. Three of those were particularly interesting and new for that part of the world:

1 To renew their vehicle license, members of the public are now able to get their vehicles road tested and inspected at several conveniently located petrol/gas stations authorized by the police department for that purpose. This saves time, as queues at the motor vehicle department are long and slow, and are open to the public only during the official hours.
2 The public can now pay for traffic violations online, by credit card, using conveniently located computer terminals situated at major shopping centers.
3 Once or twice a year, the police department launches a "safe driving campaign" where a police officer and a radio host show roam city streets trying to catch drivers doing something right. The police officer gives a reward (around $200) to those who are "caught" driving safely. The safe driver is also interviewed on live radio!

Phase 3: the values

Core values, as discussed earlier, relate to the ideology of the organization. These values guide the executive team in running the business. They take into account the interests of the stakeholders, such as the community, shareholders, customers, employees, government, and any existing networks or partnering arrangements with other parties. Thus, examples of core values in other organizations include statements of beliefs or proclamations about social responsibility, safety, health and environment, value for shareholders, quality of products and services, honesty and integrity, creativity and innovation, transparency and communication, respect and care for employees, and so on. One of 3 M's core values is innovation: "Thou shall not kill a new product idea".

During Phase 3, the police department agreed several core values; one of them was, "People come first, well before places and buildings". In fact, this core value now appears (written in large letters) on police buildings, including a prison facility! Another core value was, "The client is the boss".

In this phase, each core value is translated into action plans. For example, how will an organization implement the social responsibility core value? Here again, the How-How? method is used to convert each core value into concrete action plans, specific initiatives, and budgets. Let us say that the first "How" generates four alternative actions to be taken. Each suggested action that was generated by the first "How" would be subjected to another set of "Hows", until one reaches the hair-splitting stage where the general feeling becomes one of "just do it"! Instead, the final questions deal with the implementation and control stages, "When"? "Who"? "How well"? and "How much"?

Translating core values to action plans, programs and budgets will ensure that these values do not become hollow mottoes. It demonstrates that management is indeed committed to running the organization in line with its core values. I often tell seminar participants that these values represent the way management will act or drive during the long journey over the bridge to the future.

Phase 4: the scorecard

In Phase 4 (the scorecard), managers involved in strategy formulation would select key performance indicators (KPIs) that systematically track the progress and performance of the organization as it crosses the bridge. The KPIs are quantitative measures that keep score on key results areas or critical business activities. KPIs are used to measure performance in areas such as financial results, customer loyalty and service, innovations, market share, employee satisfaction, and so on.

Around a decade ago, Robert Kaplan and David Norton (1996, 2000) developed a management tool called the Balanced Scorecard. Their scorecard measures organizational performance across four balanced perspectives: financial, customers, internal business processes, and learning and growth. There are three prominent features of the scorecard:

1 The measures used are directly derived from the vision and strategy of the organization
2 The previous obsession with financial measures is now balanced with measures in three other areas: customers, internal business processes, and growth
3 The measures are both lagging indicators (financial measures, for example), and leading indicators that drive future financial performance (for example, innovation measures).

Quantitative measures (percentages, ratios, costs, ratings, numbers, etc.) are used to track selected key result areas, such as:

• profitability
• return on capital employed
• market share
• customer satisfaction

- customer retention
- continuous improvement initiatives
- on-time delivery
- new products
- employee competencies
- employee satisfaction
- employees' suggestion scheme.

A well-balanced scorecard may have three to four measures for each of the four perspectives, that is, between 12 to 16 measures. This, of course, varies from one organization to the other. However, developing The Balanced Scorecard system is hard work. It requires top management's commitment and perseverance; it requires teamwork and integration across organizational boundaries and roles; and it takes around 18 months to develop.

Whether an organization uses the Balanced Scorecard approach or some other tool to implement its strategy, it is imperative to keep measuring progress/milestones along the journey over the bridge. A number of appropriate KPIs, derived from the strategy, are definitely necessary to ensure that a good strategy is indeed producing the desired results. Some of the KPIs can also act as early warning systems that will enable an organization to be responsive to changes as they occur. In this way, strategy becomes dynamic and anticipatory.

Finally, I would like to remind ourselves at this time of a widely accepted observation in business management. It was well stated by Jack Welch, the former chairman of General Electric, who said, "What you measure is what you get". There is no doubt that specific, measurable, and stretching objectives and targets motivate most people; and measuring progress frequently and systematically will usually produce better results. Therefore, I would say, "What you measure gets done better".

Retirement planning

Let us now apply the concept of the bridge to developing a retirement plan. We shall use the same four phases used for strategic planning.

According to a recent survey in the USA, 95 per cent of people age 55 to 64 plan to do at least some work after they retire. That is up from 75 per cent who said the same thing four years ago. The results of this Harris Interactive poll, published in *Business Week* (17 June 2002 issue), show that 81 per cent of those polled want to continue to learn, 70 per cent want to try new things, and 63 per cent want a new hobby or interest. A very small number of people saw retirement as a time to wind down.

Of course, what you do during retirement depends on many factors; among them are your wealth, health, family, profession, and lifestyle. However, the most crucial factor is perhaps how well you have planned your retirement. It seems to me that people who do not plan view retirement as life coming to an end; while those who plan view retirement as the beginning of a new life. Ideally, retirement planning starts during midlife or earlier, but it is never too late to begin the planning process.

In their book, *The Healing Journey Through Retirement* (2000), Rich, Sampson and Fetherling suggest that there are five common phases to the process of retirement: (1) Preretirement, (2) Honeymoon, (3) Disenchantment, (4) Reorientation, and (5) Stability. Drawing on their work, I have constructed Figure 7.2 that depicts the five phases of retirement ending with three possible outcomes. I strongly feel that whether the outcome of the retirement is happy ☺, indifferent ☻, or unhappy ☹ depends, to a great extent, on how well people prepare and plan for their retirement.

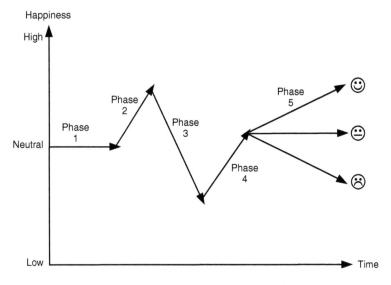

Figure 7.2 The five phases of retirement

Well, where do we begin? Once again, I found that the bridge could be a powerful tool to start developing a retirement plan. The bridge is a simple tool to use, and being visual enhances its strength. We at Meirc have conducted retirement planning workshops using it in the same manner as used in strategic thinking seminars. In the remaining part of this chapter, I will present a hypothetical retirement case to show how the bridge can be used in practice.

Phase 1: the future

As in business strategy, a person should start by attempting a draft statement of purpose or vision that describes his or her core ideology (core purpose and values), and envisioned future. The person should answer at least four questions, in consultation with his or her partner in life:

1 What do I want to do?
2 Who do I want to be?
3 Where do I want to retire?
4 When and how will I do it?

The elements to be examined by these soul-searching questions will probably include Self (physical and psychological health), Family, Friends, Profession, Financial, and Community. Some, if not most, of these will become the personal objectives or pillars that support the bridge. Systematically, apply the four questions to each of these elements. For example, "What do I want to do in terms of professional activities?" or, "What do I want to do for myself (psychologically and spiritually)?" or, "Who do I want to be (that is, my role) in terms of my family or friends?", and so on.

The third question, about where one wants to retire, is slightly different because it is dependent on the answers to the other questions. However, if financially well off, one may want to decide first where in the country or where in the world one wishes to live, and then proceed with the other questions. There is no doubt that the answers to all these questions, on all the elements, are inter-related and will influence each other. At the end, one may come up with a *draft* statement of purpose that will read something like this:

> *My aim is to play an active role in community affairs, while staying in very close touch with my extended family, friends and profession. I shall also do everything in my power to look after my health and savings for as long as possible.*

Once Phase 2 is completed, we will re-visit this draft for a reality check; that is, we will ask whether the statement of purpose is feasible, workable and realistic. Remember, the retirement plan is a living document, not one that is carved in stone, and should therefore be continuously evaluated.

Phase 2: the past, present and future scenarios

As done when formulating business strategy, there will also be a need for internal and external strategic analyses during this phase. One of the best tools to put retirement in perspective is to use the helicopter to look at the past, present and the future. This is done in two steps: First, plot your major life events on a graph starting with your first childhood memories to the present day. One axis of the graph indicates degree of happiness or mood and on the other axis is age. Think back about the most significant events (happy, indifferent, or sad), and write them on the graph, as in Figure 7.3 (you will probably need a large sheet of paper for this).

Next, think about what will make you happy in the next ten or fifteen years. Start by asking the following questions: How do I feel about my accomplishments in life up to now? What meaningful activities will fulfill some of my goals and unmet needs? What do I expect of myself in retirement? What would my family and friends expect from me as a retiree? What items would I include on my wish list? Looking forward, describe today what your retirement will look like ten years from now.

> *There is nothing you can do about your early life now, except to understand it. You can, however, do everything about the rest of your life.*
>
> (Warren Bennis, 1989)

As mentioned earlier, the major and most significant elements requiring analysis will most likely include self (health,

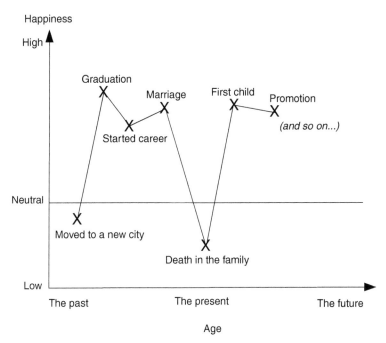

Figure 7.3 Age and happiness

psychological, spiritual, and professional competencies), family (nuclear and extended), friends, financial matters, professional interests, and role in the community or country. Now, using the SWOT analysis (*Strengths*, *Weaknesses*, *Opportunities* and *Threats*) on each of these elements, you could come up with a large number of alternative courses of action, warning signals, limiting factors and wonderful opportunities – all of which should be taken into consideration when future retirement plans are made. Life during retirement is full of choices, if only one looks for them. Let us take, as examples, three of the elements in order to demonstrate the results of the SWOT analysis.

Health

As one ages, there will be serious threats to physical and mental health especially if, upon retirement, a person *abruptly* stops working and thinking. Therefore, it becomes vital to continue exercising the body and the brain in order to reduce health problems and/or senility. This leads to the need not only to watch one's diet, but also to exercise regularly, or take up old or new hobbies. Exercise also reduces stress, and this may enhance creative thinking and may make hobbies more enjoyable. Certain hobbies may lead to making new friends and acquaintances. Therefore, one can see that a specific action may produce positive results for the other elements; in our simple example, regular exercise influences not only physical and psychological health, but may also lead to making new friends or to doing well at new creative hobbies.

Financial

Most of the literature on retirement focuses on this important element. Many books, articles and software tell us how to invest our savings, balance risk and rewards, beat inflation, and develop a budget. Of course, financial planning for retirement normally starts early in one's career, and is reviewed on a continuous basis. However, a few years prior to retirement, assistance from a financial expert is highly recommended. The expert will provide advice on how to manage your financial portfolio in order to meet your specific circumstances and ever-changing lifestyle. In general, less risky income-generating investments, such as certificates of deposit, bonds, and dividend-paying equities, are far more appropriate during retirement years. Recognizing one's strengths and opportunities (experience and wisdom; a vast network of professional and personal contacts, etc.) one can contemplate starting a new business venture during retirement or, if desirable, getting a part-time job. These possibilities should be considered for two important reasons: first, they may bring in some income; second, and perhaps more importantly, they provide the extremely healthy aspect of experiencing a *gradual* slow down in one's career.

Role in community
There are many opportunities to utilize one's areas of strengths or professional competencies, and at the same time derive satisfaction by helping others in the community. Volunteer work (if one's financial status allows it) in the community could yield many benefits such as the psychological self-fulfillment that comes from helping others, as well as the personal satisfaction of using one's competencies well after leaving work. It also keeps the brain active through working and continuous learning. Mentoring or coaching younger people in one's community is one example of volunteer work. Other examples include helping in planning or organizing community activities or special community events. It is not unusual to find retired persons volunteering their talent and time in hospitals, charities, libraries, schools, or in other social service organizations.

> *I want to be thoroughly used up when I die, for the harder I work, the more I live. Life is no brief candle for me. It is a sort of splendid torch which I have got hold of for the moment, and I want to make it burn as brightly as possible before handing it on to future generations.*
>
> (George Bernard Shaw)

Now that the strengths, weaknesses, opportunities and threats have been closely examined for each important element, it is time to revisit the statement of purpose. Taking all the facts, needs, desires, choices and constraints into consideration, you are in a better position to decide if the earlier statement of purpose is realistic and financially feasible. Here is a slightly *revised* version of the statement of purpose:

> My aim is to build and enjoy strong and meaningful relationships with my *family* and *friends*, while taking active roles in my *community* and *profession*. To accomplish this, I shall do everything in my power to manage my *savings*, and to look after my *health* (mental and physical) for as long as possible.

It is time to make decisions and begin the planning process. Decide on the pillars of the bridge, which you can derive from the statement of purpose (shown in italic type). There are six pillars in this statement: health, financial matters, family, friends, community, and profession. For each pillar, use the How-How? method to generate alternative courses of action. For example, ask yourself how you can become actively involved in community affair. Then, for *each* of the answers generated, another "How" is asked. Eventually, this method produces a great number of alternatives. Next, work out specific action plans for each of the selected high-priority alternatives. Tackle the next pillars in the same way, until you have shaped your retirement plans and expectations for the future. Remember that these plans are not carved in stone; instead, you should remain flexible and review your plans periodically. Your interests and needs will probably change, and your circumstances may change too.

> *The failure to plan for the* nonfinancial *aspects of life after work is at the root of many unhappy retirements.*

For many retirees grandparenthood is a wonderful experience that provides reinvigoration and a terrific new outlet for your energy and attention even as your devotion to your job wanes.
(From *The Healing Journey Through Retirement*,
Rich *et al.*, 2000)

Phase 3: the values

Core values change priorities as one grows in age. Figure 7.4 shows the changes in priorities for a younger person and a retiree. For our hypothetical retirees, the following are perhaps good examples of values that will guide them during their future journey over the bridge:

- love (more giving than receiving, and far more wide-spread than before)
- friendship and meaningful relationships (to compensate for years of being too involved with work and career; maybe having a reunion with friends from high school or university)
- sense of achievement/accomplishments (in areas other than work, example writing a business book or a novel!)

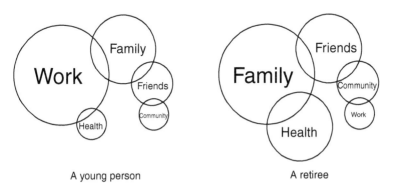

Figure 7.4 Core values and age

- giving (having been on the receiving end, it is time to give freely one's money, time, and competencies)
- self-development/life-long learning (perhaps was never completed because of work and financial obligations)
- enjoying life and leisure (now that job pressures are not there; possibly more travel and cultural events).

Phase 4: the scorecard

As in business strategy formation, the retiree would select key performance indicators (KPIs) that systematically track his or her progress and performance while crossing the bridge. In our example, the KPIs are quantitative measures that keep score on the six elements or pillars. Using the Balanced Scorecard, a number of performance measures are chosen for each of the scorecard's four perspectives (financial, customers, learning and growth, and processes). Figure 7.5 shows an example of the scorecard.

Here are some examples of KPIs for the four perspectives of the balanced scorecard.

- Financial measures: how well is the investment portfolio performing? Are there frequent or major variances in the budget?
- Customers: what were the specific activities devoted to enrich the relationship with one's spouse? Are these activities creating better quality time for both parties?
- Customers: how often, and how meaningful or enjoyable, are the get-togethers with the children (for people who have an empty nest), grandchildren (if any), extended family, and friends?
- Customers: what is the degree and frequency of involvement in community or charitable activities?

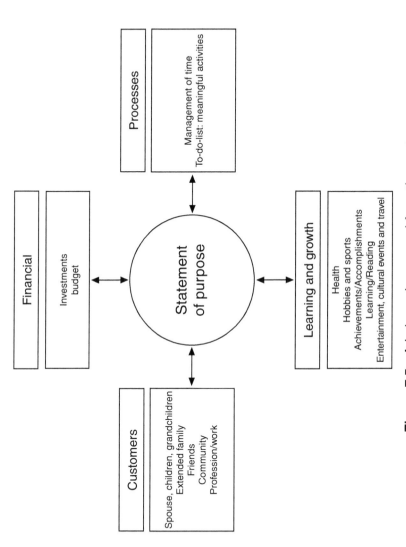

Figure 7.5 A balanced scorecard for retirement

- Customers: what tangible progress was achieved on the professional level (such as part-time work, or giving lectures on one's field of expertise)?
- Learning and growth: what is the quality of health, as judged by periodic medical check-ups and reports?
- Learning and growth: what, and how many, specific hobbies, achievements, or learning activities were started or completed?
- Learning and growth: what is the frequency and quality of entertainment, cultural events, and travel?
- Processes: how well is time managed, as judged by surplus time or boredom? In addition, how many planned activities have been postponed or cancelled, due to poor utilization of time?

Retirement can be a splendid stage in life if planned well; however, one should always be prepared for the eventual setbacks that occur as the years fly by. "Many of the unpleasant realities faced by retirees have to do with the loss of something or someone important to them: their health, the death of a loved one, or the disintegration of their family", wrote Rich *et al.* (2000) in *The Healing Journey Through Retirement*. "It's inevitable that we will experience loss and grief," they added. However, being prepared mentally and spiritually to deal with these eventualities should lessen their effect. Moreover, help from family members, friends, or specialized professionals can certainly alleviate the devastation and grief.

To bounce back from the relatively short-lived impact of tragedies, think about all the wonderful activities, dreams, or projects you have already planned, but not completed yet. Get in the helicopter, think positive, and imagine the potential rewards and happiness as you continue your successful journey across the bridge. Finally, enjoy every minute of your retirement – you deserve it!

Appendix

The 1989 and 2002 Research Studies

In 1989, Meirc Training & Consulting conducted a research study entitled *The Making of Gulf Managers*. The research looked into when, how and where managers acquire or learn managerial competencies. Over 50 organizations from the six GCC countries nominated what they considered their most successful executives and managers, and 140 of these Arab executives and managers were interviewed at length. The open-ended interview schedule appears in this Appendix. The results of these interviews were remarkable: there were ten factors that were, *repeatedly and without prompting*, mentioned by the managers interviewed – factors that managers felt led to the acquisition of certain competencies, which in turn were crucial to their managerial success. We called them "ingredients for success".

In 2002, another sample of 181 Arab executives and managers from the Gulf were asked to rank order the ten ingredients, and to add to them others from their own experience. The questionnaire used in this study also appears in the Appendix.

The results of the two studies are shown below:

The Ten Ingredients for Success

Results of the 1989 and 2002 Studies

1989 Ranking		2002 Ranking
1	Quality of Education	1
2	Exposure and Role Models	6
3	Early Responsibility	4
4	Ethics and Values	3
5	Self Development	2
6	Training Opportunities	7
7	Standards and Feedback	10
8	The Knowledge Base	5
9	Formal Career Development	9
10	A Problem-Solving Culture	8

As can be observed, the main changes in rankings were:

- Exposure and Role Models dropped from 2nd ranking to 6th.
- Self Development climbed to 2nd place from 5th.
- Standards and Feedback dropped to 10th place from 7th.
- The Knowledge Base climbed to 5th ranking from 8th.

> Charles Handy, Meirc's adviser during the 1989 research, wrote the following in his Foreword to *The Making Of Gulf Managers*:
> *I do not believe that these five ingredients are peculiar to Gulf managers; I am sure they are not; but I have never before seen their importance so clearly stated, unprompted, by people in senior management positions.*

Interview schedule used for the 1989 study

Nationality	B	K	O	Q	SA	UAE
M F						

Organization: _____ Ownership: Private Mixed Gov't

Nature of Business: _____

Number of Employees: Total: _____
Nationals: _____

Part I

	Position	Duration	Organization
1 Experience / Career:	_____	_____	_____
	_____	_____	_____
	_____	_____	_____

2 Current Position: _____

  No. Of Immediate Subordinates: _____
  No. Of Employees in your Dept. / Division: _____

3 Education: Level: _____

         Field / Specialization: _____

         Institute (name / location): _____

         Year Completed: _____

4 During the last two years, how many courses / conferences have you attended?

Events: _____   No. Of Days: _____

_____   _____

_____   _____

5 Age _____ Years
Birth position in family: Oldest   Middle   Youngest

6 Family Background: _____
Father's Occupation (Past / Present): _____
Outside Activities (Hobbies, Clubs, Own Business,
Partnership etc.): _____

Part II

1 What are your principal accomplishments / contributions in the past 2 years?
   (Check: Developing Nationals, Cost / Productivity Improvements, Organizational Objectives / Goals, etc)

2 What talents, skills and abilities helped you?

3 How did you develop these?
   (Were you born with them? When and where did you develop them? Etc.)

4 What were the factors or events that contributed to your career?
   (Check: Courses, Bosses, Job, and Crises)

5 How did you get where you are?
   (Check: Formal Appraisal, Luck, Patronage, Conspicuous Success, and Particular Abilities)

6 Are there any episodes / events / opportunities which, in retrospect, you could have handled better?

- Is there any preparation that would have helped?

Part III

1 What are the main problems the organization is facing now?

- What could be done to make things better?

2 What are the main problems **you** are facing **now** in your role?

- What could be done to make things better?

3 What skills / abilities does the organization need more of?

Part IV

Looking at your subordinates

1 What do the best of them have which the others lack?
(I.e. what do they do)

 • Is there a difference between the various nationalities? How?

2 How did the best develop these skills / abilities?
(Was it their early experiences, the organization, courses?)

3 How could the others be helped?

 • What could the organization do more of for them?

 • What could the organization do less of for them?

 • What could they themselves do?

 • What could you do?

4 In retrospect, would you / the organization have recruited different people?

- If so, what should they have looked for in these people?

- What sort of evidence would they have required (qualifications / experience) i.e. how would the organization know?

Part V

Looking at your bosses / colleagues whom you most admire
(Choose two persons):

1 What qualities / abilities / skills do you particularly admire in them?

- Please, give examples of how they demonstrated these:

- How do you think they developed / acquired these qualities / abilities / skills?

2 Looking at expatriates and nationals, what are the principal differences?

3 What are some of the characteristics of expatriates which you
 most **admire**?

> Western:
> Arab:
> Asian:

- What are some of the characteristics, which you most
 dislike?

> Western:
> Arab:
> Asian:

4 Looking at those who successfully manage expatriates, what
 do they do differently from the less successful (give specific
 instances).

Part VI

1 Managers in my organization are **not** as decisive as they
 should be:

Agree ☐   Disagree ☐

If Agree, is it because they: (please choose one answer only)

> _____ Are afraid of making mistakes
> _____ Need more data and information
> _____ Believe they need more consultation
> _____ Don't like taking risks
> _____ Other, please specify.

2 The effective manager is the one who: (circle one answer only)

   I   Usually makes his own decisions, but later explains his reasons for making these decisions.

   II   Usually consults with his subordinates before making decisions; their opinion may or may not influence his decisions.

   III Usually meets with subordinates when there is an important decision to be made. Puts the problem before them and invites discussion. Accepts the majority viewpoint as the decisions.

   IV Usually asks his subordinates to make decisions, and holds them fully accountable for the outcome of these decisions.

3 Now, for the above types of managers, please mark the one which you would prefer to work under (circle one answer only):

I   II   III   IV

4 And, to which one of the four types of managers would you say your **own** manager most closely corresponds? (Circle one answer only):

I   II   III   IV

Part VII

1 Which of the following has the greatest influence on management practices and behavior in the Gulf:

   a Friendships: _____

   b Religion: _____

   c Family Relations: _____

   d World Economy: _____

   e Government Policies: _____

   f Other, please specify: _____

   How & Why? _____

2 The biggest problems facing me and other managers in my organization are:

   _____ Subordinate lacking experience

   _____ Wastah and favoritism

   _____ Excessive rules, regulations and procedures (bureaucracy)

   _____ Interference and restrictions from outside the organization (external influences)

   _____ Lack of authority to make decisions

   _____ People have low value and respect for time
   (1= most important; and 6 = least important)

Part VIII (if person interviewed is CEO, MD or President)

1 How do you view the role of management training and development in your organization? What is its primary aim?

2 Regarding the top national managers in your organization, what do you think they need to improve their performance?

3 Who do you report to?

   How often are you in touch with him/them?

   What is the most serious problem you encounter with him/them?

Questionnaire used for the 2002 study

Nationality: _____   Age: _____

Nature of business (*i.e. oil & gas, banking, etc.*): _____

A Ingredients for success

The following were found to contribute to the acquisition of superior skills and knowledge and attitudes. Kindly rank in order of their importance to **your** success in life / management.

Please rank from 1 (most important) to 11 (least important).
Please do not skip or repeat any ranking.

_____   Training (courses and on-the-job training)

_____   Current or previous manager(s): their positive support and encouragement

_____   Practical on the job experience, and technical knowledge

_____   Quality of education received (including extra curricula activities)

_____   Self-development: a thirst for continuous learning

_____   Organizational climate and culture, which encourages learning

_____   Early responsibility (at home and at work)

_____   Exposure and role models: Learning from persons whom you respect and admire. Learning from others through exposure and travel.

_____ Formal career development programs provided by the organization

_____ Work ethics and values: hard work, integrity, commitment to work, and quality of work.

_____ Other *(Please describe):* _____

_____

B Looking back over the events and/or people in your life, which ones have been most influential in contributing to your personal or managerial success? (No names please)

1. _____

_____

2. _____

_____

3. _____

_____

C Decision making

1 **In general,** the effective manager is the one who: (circle **one** answer only)

   I   Usually makes his own decisions, but later explains his reasons for making these decisions.

  II Usually consults with his subordinates before making decisions; their opinion may or may not influence his decisions.

III Usually meets with subordinates when there is an important decision to be made. Puts the problem before them and invites discussion. Accepts the majority viewpoint as the decision.

IV Usually asks his subordinates to make decisions, and holds them accountable for the outcome of these decisions.

2 Now, for the above types of managers, please circle the **one,** which **you** would prefer to work under (circle **one** answer only)?

I   II   III   IV

3 And, to which **one** of the four types of managers would you say your **own** manager most closely corresponds (circle **one** answer only)?

I   II   III   IV

Your Manager's nationality: _____

D Expatriates

	Characteristics you admire most	Characteristics you dislike most
Western Expats	_____	_____
	_____	_____
	_____	_____
	_____	_____
	_____	_____

	Characteristics you admire most	Characteristics you dislike most
Arab Expats	_____	_____
	_____	_____
	_____	_____
	_____	_____
	_____	_____
Asian Expats	_____	_____
	_____	_____
	_____	_____
	_____	_____
	_____	_____

References

Aaker, David, *Developing Business Strategies*, 6th edition, John Wiley & Sons, 2001.

Adair, John, *Effective Motivation*, Pan Books, 1996.

Ali, A and Schaupp, D, "Value Systems as Predictors of Managerial Decision Styles of Arab Executives", *International Journal of Manpower*, Vol. 13, No. 3, 1992.

Ali, A and Swiercz, P, "The Relationship between Managerial Decision Styles and Work Satisfaction in Saudi Arabia", *Management Decision*, Vol. 23, No. 2, 1986.

Ali, A, Taqi, A and Krishnan, K, "Individualism, Collectivism, and Decision Styles of Managers in Kuwait", *Journal of Social Psychology*, Vol. 137, No. 5, 1997.

Becker, B, Huselid, M and Ulrich, D, *The HR Scorecard: Linking People, Strategy and Performance*, Harvard Business School Press, 2001.

Bennis, Warren, *On Becoming a Leader*, Addison Wesley, 1989.

Blanchard, Kenneth and Johnson, Spencer, *The One Minute Manager*, Berkeley Publishing Group, 1982.

Boyatzis, Richard, *The Competent Manager: A Model for Effective Performance*, John Wiley & Sons, 1982.

Buckingham, Marcus and Coffman, Curt, *First, Break All the Rules: What the World's Greatest Managers do Differently*, Simon & Schuster, 1999.

Buckingham, M and Clifton, D, *Now, Discover Your Strengths*, Free Press, 2001.

Business Week, 17 June 2002.

Cherniss, Cary and Goleman, Daniel (Editors), *The Emotionally Intelligent Workplace*, Jossey-Bass, 2001.

Collins, James *Good to Great: Why Some Companies Make the Leap . . . and Others Don't*, HarperCollins, 2001.

Collins, James, and Porras, Jerry, *Built to Last: Successful Habits of Visionary Companies*, HarperBusiness, 1997.

Conners, R, Smith, T and Hickman, C, *The Oz Principle: Getting Results Through Individual and Organizational Accountability*, Prentice-Hall Press, 1994.

Coon, Carleton S, *Caravan: The Story of the Middle East* (revised edition), Holt, 1958.

Cox, Charles and Cooper, Cary, *High Flyers: An Anatomy of Managerial Success*, Basil Blackwell, 1988.

Deal, Terrence and Kennedy, Allen, *Corporate Cultures*, Perseus Publishing, 2000.

de Bono, Edward, *Serious Creativity*, HarperCollins, 1992.

de Geus, Arie, *The Living Company*, paperback edition, Nicholas Brealey Publishing, 1999.

Economist, The, "A Survey of the Gulf", 23 March 2002.

Farson, R and Keyes, R, "The Failure-Tolerant Leader", *Harvard Business Review*, August 2002.

Goleman, Daniel, *Emotional Intelligence*, Bantam Books, 1995.

Goleman, Daniel, *Working with Emotional Intelligence*, Bantam Double-day, 1998.

Goleman, D, Boyatzis, R and McKee, A, *Primal Leadership: Realizing the Power of Emotional Intelligence*, Harvard Business School Press, 2002.

Gratton, Lynda, *Living Strategy: Putting People at the Heart of Corporate Purpose*, Financial Times, Prentice-Hall, Pearson Education, 2000.

Hamel, G, and Prahalad, C K, *Competing for the Future*, Harvard Business School Press, 1994.

Handy, Charles, *Understanding Organizations*, 4th edition, Penguin, 1993.

Handy, Charles, *Beyond Certainty*, Harvard Business School Press, 1996.

Hickson, David (Editor), *Exploring Management across the World*, Penguin Books, 1997.

Hofstede, Geert, *Cultures and Organizations*, McGraw-Hill, 1996.

Hofstede, Geert, *Culture's Consequences: Comparing Values, Behaviors, Institutions and Organizations across Nations*, 2nd edition, Sage Publications, 2001.

Ishikawa, Kaoru, *What is Total Quality Control? The Japanese Way*, Prentice-Hall, 1985.

Kaplan, Robert and Norton, David, *The Balanced Scorecard*, Harvard Business School Press, 1996.

Kaplan, Robert and Norton, David, *The Strategy-Focused Organization: How Balanced Scorecard Companies Thrive in the New Business Environment*, Harvard Business School Press, 2000.

Kepner, Charles and Tregoe, Benjamin, *The Rational Manager*, McGraw-Hill, 1965.

Kluckhohn, C and Murray, H, *Personality in Nature, Society and Culture*, Knopf, 1948.

Koch, Richard, *The 80/20 Principle*, Bantam Doubleday, 1998.

Kohls, L Robert, *Survival Kit for Overseas Living*, 4th edition, Nicholas Brealey Intercultural Press, 2001.

Kotter, John, *The Leadership Factor*, Free Press, 1988.

Kotter, John, *A Force for Change: How Leadership Differs from Management*, Free Press, 1990.

Kotter, John (Editor), *John Kotter on What Leaders Really Do*, Harvard Business School Press, 1999.

Kotter, J and Heskett, J, *Corporate Culture and Performance*, Free Press, 1992.

McClelland, David C, "Testing for Competence Rather than for Intelligence", *American Psychologist*, Vol. 28, No. 1, January 1973, pp. 1–14.

Majaro, Simon, *The Creative Gap*, Longman, 1988.

Margerison, Charles and Kakabadse, Andrew, *How American Chief Executives Succeed: Implications for Developing High-Potential Employees*, an AMA Survey Report, American Management Association, 1984.

Meirc Training & Consulting, *The Making of Gulf Managers*, unpublished study report distributed to Meirc's clients, 1989.

Miller, George A, "The Magical Number Seven, Plus or Minus Two: Some Limits on Our Capacity for Processing Information", *The Psychological Review*, 1956, Vol. 63.

Mintzberg, Henry, *The Rise and Fall of Strategic Planning*, Free Press, 1993.

Mintzberg, H, Ahlstrand, B and Lampel, J, *Strategic Safari: A Guided Tour Through the Wilds of Strategic Management*, Simon & Schuster, 1998.

Muna, Farid A, *The Arab Executive*, Macmillan Press, London, 1980.

Nelson, Bob, *1001 Ways to Energize Employees*, Workman Publishing Company, 1997.

Nydell, Margaret (Omar), *Understanding Arabs: A Guide for Westerners*, 3rd edition, Intercultural Press, 2002.

Osborn, Alex F, *Applied Imagination-Principles and Procedures Creative Problem-Solving*, 4th edition, Charles Scribner's Sons, 1963.

Ohmae, Kenichi, *The Mind of the Strategist*, Penguin Books, 1982.

Parry, Scott, *Evaluating the Impact of Training*, American Society for Training and Development, 1997.

Parry, Scott, *Training for Results*, American Society for Training and Development, 2000.

Pfeffer, J, *The Human Equation: Building Profits by Putting People First*, Harvard Business School Press, 1998.

Rich, P, Sampson, D and Fetherling, D, *The Healing Journey Through Retirement*, John Wiley & Sons, 2000.

Sample, Steve, *The Contrarian's Guide to Leadership*, Jossey-Bass, 2002.

Schein, Edgar, *Organizational Culture and Leadership*, Jossey-Bass, 1992.

Schein, Edgar, *The Corporate Culture Survival Guide*, Jossey-Bass, 1999.

Spencer, Lyle and Spencer, Signe, *Competence at Work: Models for Superior Performance*, John Wiley & Sons, 1993.

Sternberg, Robert, *Handbook of Creativity*, Cambridge University Press, 1999.

Trompenaars, Fons, and Hampden-Turner, Charles, *Riding the Waves of Culture*, 2nd edition, McGraw-Hill, 1997.

Welch, Jack, *Jack: Straight from the Gut*, Warner Books, 2001.

Yousef, Darwish A, "Predictors of Decision-Making Styles in a Non-Western Country", *Leadership & Organization Development Journal*, Vol. 19, No. 7, 1998.

Index

Aaker, David A 136
accountability 97–9
  definition of 98
acculturation 73
action plans 142
Adair, John 14, 43, 47
Ali, A 89
American Management
  Association (AMA) 4,
  12–13, 27
AMO equation 47–8, 56
  see also motivation;
    contributing to improved
    performance
Arabian Gulf countries
  economic development of
    78–80
  management practices in
    76–8, 90–3

problems of working in
  98–100
social pressures in 81–4
Arabic language, learning of 96–7
Aristotle 23, 33
attitudes 24–6, 35–6
  see also competencies
autocratic-consultative decision-
  making style 88–9

Balanced Scorecard methodology
  58, 143–4
  applied to retirement planning
    154–6
Barber, Margaret F 127
Becker, B 57
Bennis, Warren 12, 148
Berlin Police Department 135
Blanchard, Kenneth 37, 73–4

Boyatzis, Richard 4, 27
bridge metaphor xvii–xviii, 127–56
Buckingham, Marcus 4, 44
bureaucracy 83
Business Week 145

candle metaphor xv–xvi, xviii,
    1–22
Canon (company) 28
Capistrano, San Juan 33
career development 38–40, 82
"catching people doing things
    right" 37, 141
centralization 83
Cherniss, C 9
chief executive officers (CEOs)
    54–6
child development 16–17
Clifton, D 4
coaching 11
Coffman, Curt 4, 44
Collins, James 52, 132, 134
community work 151
    see also retirement planning
competencies
    definition of 24–6
    development of 35
    human resource management
        based on 29
    of leadership 27
    levels of 29–32
    literature on 26–8
    managerial 3–4
    measurement of 32–3
    professional 29–34
    studies of 26
    use of 34
    see also core competencies

competition, global 127–8
competitive advantage, creation
    of 28, 30
complaints from customers 102
Confucius 7, 75, 101
connections (*wastah*) 55, 83–4, 91
Connors, R 98
consultative management style
    86, 89–90
Coon, Carleton S xvii, 100
Cooper, C 12
copying by competitors 23–4, 58
core competencies 30, 33–4,
    138–9
core values 64, 129, 132–4,
    141–2
    personal 153–4
corporate culture 49, 52–4, 85
Cox, C 12
creativity in problem-solving
    107–11, 124
cross-cultural awareness 74, 92–5
cross-functional job moves
    39–40
cultural stereotyping 65
culture
    definition of 61–5
    of expatriate staff 73–4
    as a normal distribution 64–5
    theories of 61
    see also corporate culture;
        national cultures;
        organizational culture
culture shock 93–4

Deal, T 52
de Bono, Edward 108–9, 111–12,
    122–4

de Geus, Arie 106, 137
decision-making
  managerial 85–90
  and problem-solving 111–23
Delhi Police 135
Deman, Paul xiii
democratic management style xvii
deviation diagrams 117, 123–4
Disney organization 133
Drucker, Peter 40

The Economist 79–80
education, quality of 5–9, 17, 20
80/20 principle 119–20, 123–4
  see also Pareto principle
Einstein, Albert 101
Eliot, T S 75
emotional intelligence 8–9
English language, fluency in 95–6
environmental influences
  in the Arab Gulf 79–80
  on business executives 77–8
  on morale and motivation 49,
    54–6
Erasmus 9
ethics 13–14, 18–19, 21
excuses, use of 98–9
expatriate staff 60
  characteristics of 69–71
  cliquism 70–2
  in Gulf countries 79, 81, 92–7,
    100
  motivation of 72–4
  working with 68–9
expectations of staff, managers' 37
experiential learning 6–7
external analysis of organizations
  135–6, 139

external influences *see*
  environmental influences
extra-curricular activities 6–7

Farson, R 41
fathers, wisdom of 1–3
favoritism 73
Fetherling, D 145
"fifty-fifty" principle of
  motivation 14–15, 43, 47–9
financial planning, personal 150–1
fishbone diagrams 117–19, 122–4
foresight in business 138–9

Gilbert, Thomas 43
Glasgow Police Department 135
"going native" 95
Goleman, Daniel 4, 8–9, 27, 29
Gratton, L 57
Grove, Andy 47

Hakim, Ramsey xvii
Hamel, G 138–9
Hampden-Turner, Charles 61,
  63–4
Handy, Charles 12, 68, 158
health care 150
helicopter metaphor xvii, 101–25,
  136, 148, 156
  steps in learning the use of
    104–7
Heskett, J 52
Hickson, David J 67
Hofstede, Geert 61–2, 65
Honda (company) 28
How-How? methodology 120–4,
  139–42
human capital 24, 28, 42

human resources management (HRM) 24, 29, 34, 48, 57, 123
  see also competencies

iceberg metaphor xvi, xviii, 23–42
ingredients for success 3–17
  see also success
internal analysis of organizations 138–9
interpersonal relationships, aversion to 91
Ishikawa diagrams *see* fishbone diagrams
Islam 90

Johnson, Spencer 37
joint decision-making 86–7

Kakabadse, A 12–13
Kaplan, Robert 58, 143
Kennedy, A 52
Kennedy, John F 1
Kepner, Charles 107–8, 111–12
Kettering, Charles 101
key performance indicators 143–4
  for retirees 154
Keyes, R 41
Kipling, Rudyard xv, xix
Kluckhohn, C 59, 65
knowledge base 37–8
knowledge as distinct from skills 25
Koch, Richard 119
Kohls, L 94
Kotter, John 12, 38, 40–2, 52
Kuan Chung Tzu 23
Kuhn, Thomas xiii

labor unions 78–9
leadership 27, 38
learning from mistakes 41
learning opportunities 36–7, 40
learning organizations 40
localization *see* nationalization

McClelland, David 4, 14, 26–7
McKee, A 27
Majaro, Simon 102
management by objectives 62
management styles xvii, 73–7, 85–93
Margerison, C 12–13
Meirc Training & Consulting xvi, xviii, 4, 11–12, 17, 35, 51, 72–3, 76, 86, 111, 134, 146, 157–8
  interview schedules 159–72
mental maps 106
mentoring 11
Miller, George A xviii–xix
Mintzberg, Henry 128–30
mistakes, learning from 41
mosaic metaphor xvii–xviii, 75–100
motivation xvi, 14–15, 37, 43–58, 144
  contributing to improved performance 47
  of expatriate staff 72–4
  immediate manager's role in 49–52
  impact of the external environment on 54–6
  misconceptions about 44–5
  role of corporate culture in 52–4

theories of 45–6
see also self-motivation
Motorola (company) 139
multicultural managers 68–9
multicultural workforces 60
multinational organizations,
    employees of 60, 66–7
Muna, Farid A 75–6, 86
Murray, H 59, 65

national cultures 61–2, 65–72
nationalization of jobs 82–4, 100
Nelson, Bob 45–6
New York City Police
    Department 134
Nietzsche, Friedrich xiii
Norton, David 58, 143
Nydell, Margaret (Omar) 95

objectives, corporate 139–40
Ohmae, Kenichi 129–30
onion metaphor for culture 62–4
organizational culture 46, 65–72
orientation to a new culture 93–5
Osborn, Alex 108, 111

parental influence 17–19
parents' checklist 17–19
Pareto principle 119–20, 123–4
Parry, Scott 24
Pascal, Blaise 59
Pasteur, Louis 127
paternalism 91
paternalistic management style 91
performance of individual
    employees
  actions for enhancement of
    56–8

determinants of 47
prediction of 26–7
person-oriented management
    style 91
personal approach *see* person-
    oriented management style
Peter principle 23, 39
Pfeffer, J 57
police departments 134–7, 140–2
Porras, Jerry 52, 132, 134
power-sharing 85–7
Prahalad, C K 138–9
prediction of job performance
    26–7
problem-solving 102–3, 107–10
  culture of 40–1
  and decision-making 111–23
  prioritization in 117
professional competencies 29–34

Quran, Holy 90

rational aspects of thinking 111
recruiters' checklist 19–22
re-entry problem 73, 94
relationship management 27, 91
responsibility
  early taking of 11–13, 18, 21
  placed on expatriate staff 74
retirement planning 145–56
Rich, P 145, 153, 156
Roche (company) 133
role models 9–11, 14, 18, 20
rote learning 6

Sample, Steven 44
Sampson, D 145
scandals, corporate 97

Schaupp, D 89
Schein, Edgar 46, 52
selection of staff 44–5
self-awareness and self-
     management 27
self-development 15–17, 19, 22, 40
self-motivation 44, 47, 53–4
seven, the magical number xix
Shaw, George Bernard 151
Simmonds, Ken 129
Singapore Police Force 135
skills and skill shortages 25, 34,
     81–2
social awareness 27
Sony (company) 28, 133, 138
Spencer, L 4, 27
statements of purpose, personal
     147, 151–2
stereotyping 65, 72
Sternberg, R 110
strategic management and
     planning 128–30
strategic thinking 139–40
strategy, definition of 128–9
success, managerial, ingredients
     of 5–22, 35–42
Sun-Tzu 127
Swiercz, P 89
SWOT analysis 136–8, 149–51

taxation 79
technology transfer 96
thinking hats 109, 122–4
     see also de Bono

thinking processes 111
3M (company) 132–3, 142
time, attitudes to 65, 84, 95
Toronto Police 135
Toyota (company) 28
TPU and motivation 51–2
training opportunities 36–7
transit lounge metaphor xvi, xviii,
     59–74
Tregoe, B 107–8, 111–12
tripod metaphor xvi, 43–58
Trompenaars, Fons 61–4

unemployment 81, 84
Unilever (company) 133

values 13–14, 18–19, 21
     see also core values
Van Buren, A 1
vision, definition of 132
vision statements 134–5, 139–40
visual concepts 124, 130
volunteer work 151

"walking the talk" 15, 54
wastah see connections
Watson, Thomas Sr. 41
Welch, Jack 14, 140, 144
women, in the Gulf 79, 82, 100
work ethic 13
     see also ethics

Yousef, Darwish A 89

For Product Safety Concerns and Information please contact our EU
representative GPSR@taylorandfrancis.com
Taylor & Francis Verlag GmbH, Kaufingerstraße 24, 80331 München, Germany